THE NEW WINDMILL SERIES

General Editors: Anne and Ian Serraillier

13

GREEKS AND TROJANS

This companion book to *Men and Gods* (no. 13 in this series) relates the chief episodes in the story of the Trojan War. Part translation, part adaptation, it is based mainly on the *Iliad*. While remaining sensitive to the poetry of the Greek original, it is also notable for the pace and excitement of the story-telling.

THE BATTLE BY THE SHIPS

REX WARNER

GREEKS
and
TROJANS

ILLUSTRATED BY
EDWARD BAWDEN

HEINEMANN EDUCATIONAL BOOKS
LONDON

Heinemann Educational Books Ltd
22 Bedford Square, London WC1B 3HH

LONDON   EDINBURGH   MELBOURNE   AUCKLAND
HONG KONG   SINGAPORE   KUALA LUMPUR   NEW DELHI
NAIROBI   JOHANNESBURG   IBADAN
EXETER (NH)   KINGSTON   PORT OF SPAIN

ISBN 0 435 12013 1

FIRST PUBLISHED 1951
FIRST PUBLISHED IN THE NEW WINDMILL SERIES 1952
REPRINTED 1956, 1959, 1960, 1961, 1962 (twice), 1967,
1969 (twice), 1971, 1974, 1978, 1981

Greeks and Trojans is included in this series
by kind permission of Messrs. MacGibbon & Kee Ltd

TO GEORGE

PRINTED IN GREAT BRITAIN BY BUTLER AND TANNER LTD
FROME AND LONDON

CONTENTS

BOOK THREE

The Fall of Troy

ILLUSTRATIONS

PREFACE

IN THIS volume I have attempted to relate the main
episodes in the story of the Trojan War. Naturally the
greater part of the narrative comes from the "Iliad," and
so Book Two is much the longest portion of this work. In
this Book I have sometimes translated and sometimes
altered or adapted the Greek of portions of the "Iliad," and
here I should record a debt of gratitude to the modern
translation made by E. V. Rieu, a translation which I have
often found helpful. Book One describes the origins of the
war and Book Three continues the narrative from the death
of Hector to the escape of Aeneas. Some of these earlier
and later stories are difficult to fit in with the main story as
told by Homer. Odysseus, for instance, is a great hero in
Homer, but something of a crook both in Sophocles and in
Virgil. In Homer there is only a brief mention of the
Judgment of Paris and no mention at all of Leda and the
Swan. Yet these stories are so well known and have so often
inspired poets and painters that it seemed wrong to leave
them out. So also I thought with regard to such characters
as Memnon and Penthesilea who can scarcely be delineated
in words but who have formed the subjects of well known
paintings on Greek vases.

R. W.

BOOK ONE

THE GREEKS AND
THE TROJANS

DIOMEDES, PANDARUS, AENEAS, AND APHRODITE

THE CITY OF TROY

NOT FAR from the sea coast in the north of Asia Minor once stood the city of Troy. Here was fought the great war between the Greeks and the Trojans, a war in which Achilles and Hector and so many other heroes lost their lives but won eternal fame. The gods also took part in the war, some on the side of the Trojans and some on the side of the Greeks. For ten years the struggle was undecided and the rivers of Troy, the Scamander and the Simois, ran red with blood. In the end the city was destroyed but of the Greeks many who had escaped the battle died on their homeward voyage, or wandered for long years in stormy seas along inhospitable coasts, or at their return found murder and treachery waiting for them in their own homes. It is said that the war was for a woman's sake, the sake of Helen, the wife of Menelaus. Yet the rivalry of the gods, the folly and ambition of men played their part also.

The great walls of Troy were built by the gods. Once Apollo was banished from heaven by Zeus, the King of the Gods. There are many stories of Apollo's doings on earth, but what concerns us here is that he, with Poseidon, the god of the sea, built the high walls of Troy for the Trojan King Laomedon. This treacherous and ungrateful king, in spite of the kindness he had received, refused, when the work was done, to pay the reward which he had promised. Then Apollo sent a pestilence among the people of Laomedon, and Poseidon sent from the sea a great monster which ravaged the crops and easily destroyed the warriors who were sent against it. In the distress of his people Laomedon consulted the oracle and was told that the gods' anger could not be appeased except by the sacrifice each year of a Trojan maiden to the monster. So each year a maiden was chosen by lot and then, in spite of her tears and the tears of her parents and her friends, was taken to the sea shore and left there to be devoured by the great beast that came out of the sea.

For five years the city paid this terrible penalty for the treachery of its king, and in the sixth year the daughter of the king himself, Hesione, was chosen to be sacrificed. Now indeed Laomedon and his wife wished that greater respect had been paid to the gods, and that the promise had been fulfilled. Yet the gods were merciful, and in their misery help was at hand.

At this time the great hero Herakles with a band of his companions was returning from his expedition against the Queen of the Amazons, whose girdle he had taken from her by the orders of his cowardly master, King Eurystheus. As his ship put in to Troy he saw on the beach the sad procession which was accompanying Hesione to her doom, and he asked the reason for the black clothes and the wailing and the lamentation. King Laomedon told him of the danger in which his daughter stood and Herakles undertook to fight with the monster on the condition that, if he was successful, the king would give him a number of his fine horses, swift as the wind, great spirited animals that raced over the plains of Troy. Laomedon gladly and willingly agreed, and Herakles threw aside his lion skin cloak, gripped his club in his strong hands and made ready for battle.

Soon, at a great distance from the shore, one could see the blue water churned white as the beast approached. Its great head towered above the waves and through its rows of enormous teeth it belched out the foam. Herakles stood firm and indeed stepped forward to the shore, meeting the monstrous animal in the shallow water. With one blow of his club he stunned it; then, thrusting his sword into its heart he stained all the water scarlet with its blood.

Hesione was saved and now one would have thought that Laomedon in gratitude for his daughter's safety and warned already by the previous punishment for his treachery, would ungrudgingly have given the hero his reward. It seems however that many people are unable to learn from experience. Once again Laomedon refused to carry out his part of the bargain. Herakles then, with his companions, attacked the city of Troy, took it by storm, killed King Laomedon and took the whole of his family prisoner. He gave Hesione to his follower Telamon who by her had a son, Teucer, who later was to fight with the Greeks against his mother's country in the great Trojan War. As for the other descendants of King Laomedon, only one was allowed to remain. This was the young boy Priam who was to become the last and the greatest of the Trojan kings. Herakles, before he sailed away, accepted a ransom for this boy and placed him on his father's throne.

So for many years, under the rule of King Priam and his Queen Hecuba, Troy grew ever richer, stronger and more prosperous. Priam made alliances with the neighbouring princes; he strengthened the vast fortifications of his city; ships that passed along the coast paid tribute to his officers; his kingdom became one of the mightiest in the world.

Priam and Hecuba had nineteen children who, when they grew up, became famous princes and princesses. Among them none was more famous than Hector both for his strength and skill in war and for his goodness of heart and loyalty to his friends. In these qualities he had no rival unless it was Priam's nephew Aeneas, whom Aphrodite loved, since he was her son. For she, the goddess of love, had fallen in love herself with the young Prince Anchises of the Trojan royal house. Anchises was feeding his sheep along the slopes of Mount Ida, the mountain that towers above the city of Troy, when the goddess, charmed by his beauty, visited him and by him became the mother of Aeneas, the hero who long afterwards and after many adventures was to found the great race of the Romans.

With such princes and warriors, with so many allies, such wealth and such magnificence, it might have seemed that the city of Troy was securely fixed in power and happiness and that it would last for ever, standing proudly in the plain below Mount Ida, with the holy rivers Simois and Scamander crossing the plain, tall and mighty with its towers, its huge walls and its tremendous gates. But this was not the will of the gods.

II

THE JUDGMENT OF PARIS

IT IS said that before Priam's son, Paris, was born, his mother Hecuba dreamed that she would give birth not to a baby but to a flaming torch. Terrified by her dreams she consulted the prophets and soothsayers of Troy. Their answers were all the same—that the child whom she would bear would be the destruction of his city and of his family.

It seemed to Priam and to Hecuba better that the infant should perish than that he should bring such a doom on themselves, their people and their other children. Yet they had not the heart to kill the child: instead they gave him, soon after his birth, to a shepherd and told him to leave the baby on the rocky heights of Mount Ida, where the wild beasts and birds would soon find him and devour him.

Yet this was not what happened. Whether it was this shepherd himself that spared the boy and brought him up, or whether it was other shepherds or herdsmen on the mountain who had mercy on the small exposed body, Paris was certainly saved, although for long his parents did not know it. He grew up among the country people whose living was on Mount Ida, and as he grew up he stood out among the rest of the young boys because of his strength and his beauty. He was skilful in the use of his weapons and would spend long hours hunting wild boars in the thickets or lions on the bare slopes of the mountain. Particularly was he skilled in archery, and at every competition he would take the first prize. As he grew stronger, so he

grew more beautiful. He married one of the mountain
nymphs, Oenone, who was as beautiful as himself, who had
a perfect knowledge of all healing herbs and who loved
him most tenderly. So on this mountain with a divine
creature for his wife, famous among the humble folk who
surrounded him, Paris might have lived his whole life
through in happiness. Yet it seems that he was not con-
tented with what he had, and he was drawn into disaster by
a conflict among the gods themselves.

For at this time there took place the famous wedding
between the sea goddess Thetis and the great Greek hero
Peleus. Of Thetis it had been foretold that she was destined
to bear a son even mightier than his father. Zeus himself
had desired her for his wife, but he feared a son who might
one day take his power from him and so it was to a mortal
that Thetis was married. The prophecy indeed came true
since the son of Peleus and Thetis was Achilles himself, the
greatest warrior and fastest runner of his time, one against
whom not even Hector could stand in battle.

To the wedding all the gods and goddesses were invited
except one. This was Eris, the goddess of strife and discord,
and she determined to be revenged for being overlooked.
This was the method she chose. She stole up to the great
banqueting hall where the wedding feast was being held
and she threw into the middle of the assembled guests a
golden apple on which were inscribed the words: "A prize
for the most beautiful." Quarrelling immediately broke
out among the goddesses, since each one considered herself
to be more beautiful than the next. In the end, however,
the inferior goddesses had to withdraw their claims. Three
remained, none of whom would give way to the others.
These goddesses were Hera, the wife of Zeus, Athene, the
goddess of wisdom, and Aphrodite, the goddess of love.
Not even the gods themselves dared to judge between these
powerful and embittered goddesses. Instead they elected
to leave the decision in the hands of a mortal, and the mortal

they chose for the task was Paris, who watched the sheep-folds on Mount Ida.

Quickly the goddesses prepared themselves for the contest in beauty. They came to the plain of Troy, and first they bathed themselves in the river Scamander, which the gods call "Xanthus" or "the yellow river." After they had perfumed themselves and dressed their hair, they came together, all naked, to Mount Ida, to the wooded glen in the mountain where Paris was watching his sheep. And as the goddesses trod over the grassy ground, in clear sunlight or in the dappled shade of trees, the air, even where the sun shone, seemed to grow brighter; birds sang more cheerfully among the leafy thickets; wild beasts, boars and lions looked reverently from their lairs as the divine shapes of beauty passed them by. All nature was glad. Only the nymph, Oenone, in a kind of foreboding trembled at what she saw and hid her face behind her hands as the tears flooded to her eyes.

Paris himself, with his mortal eyes, could scarcely bear the vision of such loveliness and of such power. But the goddesses reassured him. Though they seemed unwilling to speak to each other, they spoke readily to him. They told him to look at them well and then to make his decision which one of the three was most beautiful. Then as Paris, abashed by the difficulty of making the choice, still hesitated, each began to attempt to influence his choice by offering him rewards. First Hera spoke and promised him that, if he gave the prize to her, she would give him power over men and over cities; his armies should conquer wherever they went; his name should be famous throughout the world; nothing, she told him, can give a man more satisfaction than absolute power which brings with it also all kinds of experience and enjoyment.

Paris, as he looked at the goddess's fine brow and great resolute eyes, felt that she spoke the truth and was on the point of giving her the apple. But Athene, fixing him with her grey eyes, calm and fearless, spoke scornfully and said: "Power without Wisdom will always lead to certain disaster. But Wisdom will bring you not only its own delights but power as well, should you desire to have it. What I offer you is the most precious thing of all—Knowledge of men and of all arts, knowledge of yourself, the power to choose rightly between opinions and between actions. It is this wisdom which, more than all else, men learn to wish that they had or that they could acquire."

With such dignity and certainty did Athene speak that once more Paris hesitated. How could he disobey a goddess in whose clear eyes he read such assurance?

But now the laughter-loving Aphrodite turned to him and smiled as she shook back from her head the loose tresses of her golden hair. "Paris," she said, "the life of mortals is a short one and there are few pleasures that are certain. But in love certainly there can be pleasure with no pain attached. What I offer you is love, the love of the most beautiful woman whom the world holds. Helen is her name and she is half divine since Zeus himself was her father. All the heroes of the Greeks came to be her suitors and now she lives in Sparta with her husband Menelaus. Give the prize to me and Helen shall be yours."

As he listened to the goddess's urgent voice and looked into her smiling eyes, Paris felt as though his bones were melting within him. Of power and of wisdom he could not think at all; nor did he even remember his own wife, the nymph Oenone, who at that very moment among the trees of Ida was weeping in a hidden glade. All his desire was to possess Helen for his own. He took the golden apple in his hand and gave it to Aphrodite, who laughed as she received the prize, while the other two goddesses, stern and angry, turned both from her and from Paris who had rejected them.

This judgment was the beginning of endless sufferings, of death, wounds, treachery and destruction both for the Trojans and for the Greeks. But at the time neither Paris himself nor any of those thousands whom his actions would bring to ruin had any knowledge of what the future would bring. It is said indeed that Oenone, who had the gift of prophecy, told Paris that, if he went to Greece, the result of his action would be certain disaster for himself and for his people, that he would die in battle and ask in vain for the help of her healing arts. But Paris gave no consideration either to Oenone's love for him or to her warnings. He left her behind him on Mount Ida and came into the city of Troy, certain that in some way or other the promise of Aphrodite would be fulfilled.

In the great city his beauty, and his prowess made him remarkable even among the princes and warriors who were his brothers. Some of these he defeated in an athletic contest, and then they say that Cassandra, his sister and a prophetess, by closely questioning him about his age and his upbringing was able to show that he was indeed the boy whom Priam and Hecuba had believed to have died upon the mountains. Seeing him now in the beauty of his youth, his old parents forgot the warning of the oracles and felt nothing but joy in recovering so fine a son. Every honour was given to Paris, and in the end King Priam gave him a fleet of ships and allowed him to sail into Greek waters. The purpose of the voyage was supposed to be in order to bring back Hesione, the sister of Priam, whom Herakles and his men had taken away. But this was not the purpose of Paris. Instead he sailed to southern Greece and came to Sparta, the city where Menelaus was King and Helen Queen.

But now the story must be interrupted to tell of Menelaus and Agamemnon, his great brother, who ruled over the city of Mycenae which is called "golden."

III

THE HOUSE OF ATREUS

WHEN CLOSE to Greece Paris's ships must have gone through the blue waters of the sea that is called the Myrtoan Sea. This sea took its name from Myrtilus, a charioteer, who had once been basely murdered by Pelops, the grandfather of Agamemnon and Menelaus. As we shall see, very many misfortunes came upon this family, which in every generation offended the gods by their pride and men by their unjust dealings. Of them all Menelaus alone lived a blameless life and he in the end was rewarded by the gods with a place in the Islands of the Blessed.

The founder of the family was Tantalus, the wealthy king of Lydia, who was admitted to the banquets of the gods. But in his wicked pride he wished to discover whether the gods could be deceived and he thought out a cruel and a barbarous plan. He killed his own son, Pelops, cut the body up, cooked it and served it to the gods as meat. The goddess Demeter was present at the feast and she at this time was mourning for her daughter Persephone, whom Pluto, god of the lower world, had carried away. In her grief she was distraught and, without noticing what she did, she ate a portion of the boy's shoulder. The other gods and goddesses, in no way deceived, had risen from the table in anger and disgust. Tantalus himself had partaken of their own food and so was immortal; yet his immortality could not save him from eternal punishment. Now in the deepest prison of Hell, where the great criminals suffer continually for their sins, Tantalus remains tortured by hunger and by thirst. Branches loaded with fruit sway before his eyes; but when he reaches out a hand to relieve his hunger, the fruit moves always out of his reach. He stands by a pool of shining water; but when he bends down to take even a little in his hands to cool his burning thirst, instead of the pool he sees ashes or desert sand.

When the gods had punished the guilty, they proceeded to restore the innocent. They gave Pelops back his life and instead of the shoulder which had been devoured they gave him a shoulder of ivory. This shoulder had miraculous powers and by its touch alone could cure wounds that otherwise would have been mortal.

So Pelops grew up in Lydia, a country that is near the boundaries of Troy. Yet it was fated for him to found his kingdom elsewhere. Long before the time of Priam a Trojan King conquered Lydia, and Pelops with his followers came to southern Greece. Here at the court of King Oenomaus of Pisa he saw the King's daughter Hippodamia and he immediately fell in love with her. His wealth and his person made him one whom any father might wish to have as a son-in-law. But King Oenomaus wished to keep his daughter to himself and would give her to no man who could not first beat him in a chariot race. The penalty for losing the race was death, and already thirteen young men, suitors of Hippodamia, had perished by her father's hand. His horses were as swift as the wind and, as he swept past his defeated rivals, he would plunge into their bodies his heavy spear and leave them dead upon the level plain.

Pelops knew the danger that stood between him and the bride whom he desired. He accepted the contest, but previously he bribed Myrtilus, the King's charioteer, to loosen the linchpins of his master's chariot, so that at the first bend of the course the chariot would be dashed in pieces. He knew that if he could survive so long, the victory would be his.

It was the habit of King Oenomaus to give a short start to those who raced with him, and, as Pelops, with his chariot in front, sped towards the bend of the long course he prayed to the gods that he might reach it in time. Behind him he could hear the thundering hoofs of his opponent's horses, and as he reached the bend he seemed to feel their breath upon his back. In a second or two, he knew, the heavy javelin would be through his body. But he turned the bend, and hardly had he turned it when he heard from behind him cries and the noise of the breaking up of the cruel king's chariot. The wheels had sprung from the axle. Oenomaus, the reins tangled round his waist, was being dragged over the stony ground by wild horses that he could no longer control. So this fierce king was killed. Pelops took Hippodamia as his bride and in the place where the race had been held he instituted for all Greece the famous Olympic Games.

But when Myrtilus, the charioteer, came to claim the reward that had been promised to him, Pelops treacherously refused. He killed Myrtilus and threw his body into the sea that bears his name.

In spite of this wicked deed Pelops continued to prosper. With Hippodamia as his wife he founded a great kingdom, so great indeed that all the southern part of Greece is to this day called after his name the Peloponnese or "Island of Pelops." Not only Pisa, but the great cities of Mycenae and of Argos came into his control. His power now was greater than it had ever been in Asia. Yet in his family he was not fortunate, though he died before he could see the terrible rivalry and the monstrous doings of his sons.

The eldest of these sons was Atreus, and it was he who inherited the great Kingdom that Pelops had founded. But his younger brother Thyestes continually plotted against him. Atreus' wife was called Aerope, and his sons by her were the famous princes Agamemnon and Menelaus. After their birth however Thyestes by his cunning acts won the love of his brother's wife, lived secretly with her and by her became the father of children. For some time the guilty secret was hidden, but in the end it was discovered. At first Atreus, in his fury, banished his brother from his dominions; but soon he thought of a revenge more cruel than banishment. He pretended that he wished to be reconciled with his brother and invited him to a feast in order to celebrate the occasion. Thyestes came, never suspecting the wicked outrage which Atreus intended to commit.

At the feast the two brothers spoke as though they had become friends, but at the end of the feast Atreus called a servant and ordered him to show Thyestes the dish from which he had just been eating. Thyestes looked and saw with horror that the meat which he had devoured was the flesh of no animal but human flesh. Atreus had killed the children of Aerope and Thyestes and had given the bodies, made unrecognisable in the cooking, to their father to eat. They say that at this deed, so horrible in its cruelty and impiety, the Sun itself turned backwards in its course, shrinking from the abominations of men.

Thyestes, when he realised what had been done to him, sprang up and overturned the table with his foot. Before he fled he called down a great curse on the house of Atreus, praying the gods that the blood of his children should be paid for by the blood of the children of Atreus, that treachery should follow treachery, that the very stones of the palace of Mycenae should preserve the memorial of the evil that had been done there. Then he fled from the Peloponnese, still fearing his brother's hatred, and in northern Greece, again through guilty love, he became the father of a son who was named Aegisthus. Much later Aegisthus returned to the plain of Argos and to Mycenae. There, though he was cowardly and scheming like his father, he helped to bring ruin on the greatest of Atreus' sons and on others as well.

All this, however, was still in the future. For the rest of his life, Atreus lived in security, though always he dreaded the effects of his brother's curse. On his death his Kingdom passed to Agamemnon and Menelaus. Agamemnon kept the fortress of Mycenae whose vast gates are flanked by great lions of stone, a fortress that governs the fertile plain of Argos and guards the mountain passes to the north. There he lived, the richest and most powerful of the Kings of Greece, with innumerable servants, armies and fleets at his command. His wife was the proud and beautiful Clytemnestra, and it was through his wife that in the end he was, in the moment of his glory, betrayed.

His brother, the golden-haired Menelaus, had Sparta for his Kingdom and there, beside the reedy banks of the river Eurotas, he lived with his wife Helen, whom all the youth of Greece had sought in marriage. It was to Sparta that Paris came with his Trojan ships.

IV

HELEN

THE BIRTH of Helen was in every way remarkable. Her mother was Leda, wife of King Tyndarus of Sparta, a woman noted for her great beauty. Her father was, or rather appeared to be, a swan.

One day Leda was bathing in the waters of the river Eurotas. Zeus, the King of the Gods, saw her there and loved her. In order to be close to her he took upon himself the form of a white swan and he made a fierce eagle pretend to be pursuing him. Leda had pity on the fugitive bird and took him into her arms, while the eagle checked its flight and wheeled away screaming over the mountains. It was not immediately that Leda knew that the great white bird with powerful wings who had sheltered in her embrace was no bird at all, but the mightiest of the gods. In the end, however, when the time came for her to give birth, she gave birth not to babies but to two white eggs. Out of one of the eggs came Helen and her brother Polydeuces, or Pollux, as he is often called; from the other egg came Castor and Clytemnestra. It is said that Helen and Polydeuces were the children of Zeus and that the others were children of Leda's husband Tyndarus; but on this point there are several different accounts. We know certainly that Polydeuces and Castor, after many adventures on earth, were in the end received among the gods and given the power to answer the prayers of sailors in stormy seas. Sometimes they appear above the masts of ships like balls of fire; sometimes they ride on their white horses over the lessening foam.

As for Helen and Clytemnestra, they married the greatest kings of Greece. Clytemnestra married Agamemnon, the son of Atreus, and lived with him in the rocky fortress of Mycenae. By him she had three children, all of whom were, though in different ways, both famous and unfortunate. There were two daughters, Iphigeneia and Electra, and one son, Orestes. Until the time of the Trojan War everything prospered with her and with Agamemnon in their kingdom.

But when the time came for Helen to be married, the fame of her divine beauty had so spread throughout Greece that there was scarcely one of the heroes of the time who did not come to Sparta to ask for her as his bride. From the far north of Greece came Achilles, son of the goddess Thetis, the greatest warrior in the world. Of the youth and childhood of Achilles many stories are told, and two of these may be mentioned here. He was greatly loved by his mother who wished to make him immortal and, in order to do so, used to bathe his body in the waters of the river Styx. But, whether because it was the will of the gods or because of her own carelessness, she omitted to bathe his heels, since she held him by the heels as she dipped the body into the water. Thus there was one part of his body, and one alone where Achilles might be wounded. Later, it is said, Thetis enquired from Zeus himself what the fate of her son would be, and Zeus told her that he might either live a long and prosperous life in his kingdom, enjoying both peace and happiness, but not to be greatly remembered after his death, or else he could have a short life, but one which would be for ever famous amongst men. It is said that Thetis begged her son to choose a long life for himself, but that he preferred glory above every other happiness and chose instead to live for a short time a life that would make him always famous.

Many others besides Achilles came to be the suitors of Helen. There was Antilochus, the strong son of Nestor, who lived in sandy Pylos. Nestor was the oldest and wisest of the kings of his time, and in his youth had known the great heroes of the past, Herakles, Theseus, Jason and the rest. In the Peloponnese he was only less powerful than Agamemnon himself. Ajax came also, a giant of a man and perhaps the strongest alive. With him came from Salamis his brother Teucer, the famous archer. Philoctetes came, carrying the bow and arrows of Herakles which, when he was a mere boy, he had been given by the hero just before his death. Yellow-haired Menelaus came from Sparta. And from the rocky island of Ithaca came Odysseus, the wisest and most resourceful of all men. So many indeed were the heroes, sons of kings and of gods, who desired to marry Helen that Tyndarus and Leda were at a loss to know how they would choose from them all a husband for Helen without giving offence to all the others who were passed over. It is said that in the end the wise advice of Odysseus was followed. What Odysseus suggested was that Helen should be allowed to choose freely herself from among her suitors the man whom she wished to marry, but that, before she made her choice, they should all swear on oath to protect her and her husband, whoever that might be, in the years to come. This plan was agreed upon, and Helen chose Agamemnon's brother, the yellow-haired Menelaus. It is said that in return for his good advice Odysseus received for himself as his wife the good and beautiful niece of Tyndarus, the famous Penelope.

So the heroes went back to their countries, having sworn that, if the need should arise, they would come together for the defence of Helen and of Menelaus. These two lived in Sparta happily together. One daughter was born to them, Hermione. They together with the rest of the Greeks and the Trojans might have lived out their lives in calm and in happiness, had it not been for the rivalry of the three goddesses and the faithless choice of Paris.

When Paris, with his Trojan followers, came to Sparta, they were received kindly and hospitably by Menelaus and his wife. In the king's great banqueting hall tables were set before them, loaded with meat and bread. The wine was mixed in golden cups and after the dinner was over a poet sang to the company of the great deeds done in old days, of the labours of Herakles, of the death of Meleager and of the Golden Fleece. The poet did not know that he was witnessing the beginning of a story which later would become more famous than any of these.

So, after the feasting and the conversation, they retired to bed. Menelaus and Helen lay down in their room at the back of the gorgeous banqueting hall. For Paris and his companions beds were made beneath the high porch of the building. Sheep-skin rugs were spread for them, with purple coverlets. So they rested after their journey, but Paris stayed awake. He had seen Helen and found her more beautiful even than he had imagined. He thought nothing of the hospitality which had been shown to him, or of the dangers which he might bring upon his native land. For many days he stayed within the palace and then, when Menelaus was absent on a voyage to Crete, he took Helen away with him, set her on board his ship and, swifter than pursuit, made his way to Troy. Whether Helen came with him willingly or not, we do not know; but in Troy she was received as though she were his wife. The old King Priam welcomed her and supported his son in his act of theft, partly for the sake of Helen herself, partly because of Hesione, his sister, whom the Greeks had taken from him. Nevertheless in receiving Paris and Helen within his walls, Priam was receiving a curse which would utterly destroy him and his children and his city. It was as though a lighted torch had come within the town, indeed the very thing that the oracle had foretold.

V

THE GREEKS SET SAIL FOR TROY

WHEN MENELAUS returned from Crete to Sparta and found that Paris had treacherously taken his wife from him, he felt that all the joy in his house had departed. The statues in his high golden hall seemed to stare at him with lifeless eyes; the empty place in the bed where Helen had slept seemed to reproach him. Soon he determined on revenge and his great brother Agamemnon was not slow to come to his help. These two first gathered together their armies and their fleets, and at the same time they sent messages to the other kings and chieftains of Greece, commanding some and urging others to join in the expedition against Troy.

Kings and warriors came together in such numbers that it would be tiresome to mention all their names. But there are some names which must be mentioned. From the far north of Greece came Achilles with fifty ships. He led into battle his own fierce troops, the Myrmidons, and he was accompanied by his friend Patroclus. He knew before he went that in this war he would lose his life, but this knowledge only made him fight the more fiercely and strive the more earnestly after glory. Among the shadowy mountains of his native land he left behind his old father, Peleus. He had a son too, Neoptolemus, who later was himself to fight at Troy.

From Ithaca and the islands of the western coast came the wise Odysseus. He left behind him his wife Penelope and his infant son Telemachus. He did not know that it would be twenty years before he saw them again, and that then, when he did see them, he would find riotous princes usurping his house and his rights. There was none of the Greeks so full of resource as Odysseus or so good in counsel, unless it were, perhaps, the old King Nestor who came from sandy Pylos with his army and his strong son, Antilochus.

The great warrior Diomedes led an army from the enormous walls of the city of Tiryns, from the coasts surrounding this famous citadel and from the islands that lie beyond the gulf of Argos. He was one who, as we shall see, was not afraid to fight against the gods themselves.

From the island of Salamis came the giant Ajax, with his brother Teucer, the famous archer. Their father was Telamon, the friend of Herakles, who in the past had taken Priam's sister Hesione from Troy.

Eighty ships came from the great cities of Crete. They were under the command of the famous spearman Idomeneus. From Rhodes too and the other islands came ships and men; indeed from every great city, from Athens and from golden Orchomenos, from the plains and from the mountains, warriors came together for the war. The whole force was under the command of Agamemnon, whose kingdom was the greatest, and no such a force had ever before been gathered.

When all preparations were made the fleet assembled at Aulis, a harbour in central Greece, near the island of Euboea. Here, at Aulis, before the fleet sailed for Troy there occurred an event which might well have discouraged the Greeks, and here too Agamemnon was persuaded to do a deed which in the end was to bring upon himself and his family the greatest misfortunes.

Something which appeared certainly to be a miracle happened while the Greeks were waiting at Aulis for favourable winds to carry them over the sea to Troy. It was when the Greek leaders were sacrificing to the gods in a holy place where a bright spring gushed out of the ground beneath a plane tree. Suddenly they saw a large snake with blood-red markings on its back. It glided out from beneath the altar and made for the plane tree. In the tree there were some young fledgling sparrows who had struggled to the end of one of the branches and were cowering there, eight of them, or nine, counting the mother bird. All these little birds, with their pitiful chirping voices, the snake devoured, and then, as the mother bird came flying round, crying for her lost brood, the snake seized her by the end of her wing and ate her too. The gods then clearly revealed that this was an omen; for when the snake had eaten the young sparrows and their mother, it was turned itself to stone.

The Greeks stared at the sight in astonishment. Then Calchas, the prophet and soothsayer to the army, spoke. "Do not be afraid," he said, "you long-haired Greeks. Zeus himself has given us a sign. He took long to send it and we shall have to wait long for its fulfilment. Just as this snake has eaten the eight nestlings and the mother, to make nine, so we shall be for nine years fighting against Troy. But in the tenth year the city, with its broad streets, will be in our hands."

As the army listened to Calchas, some believed his words and thought with dismay that they would be, even if they survived the fighting, so long separated from parents, wives and children. Others could not believe that so great an armament as theirs could fail to be quickly successful even against Troy's high walls and against the valour of her defenders.

Yet difficulties met them at the very beginning. For long months they waited in Aulis for winds to fill their sails and carry them across the sea. It is said that the goddess Artemis was angry with the Greeks because Agamemnon had unknowingly killed a stag that was sacred to her. However this may be, no winds blew and the fleet was becalmed. At the prows of the beaked and painted ships the cables began to rot away. Food became scarce; the army grew weary of waiting; and soon the storms would begin to trouble the sea and the safe season for sailing be past. Once again Calchas spoke to the generals. "There is only one way," he said, "by which the goddess's anger can be appeased. It is a hard way, but it is a way that must be taken, if we are ever to set our feet on the windy plains of Troy. What the goddess demands is a sacrifice, and the sacrifice must be nothing less than the eldest and favourite daughter of King Agamemnon."

The prophet ceased speaking, and there was a hush in the council, as kings and chieftains looked in each other's faces and in the face of Agamemnon himself.

As for Agamemnon he thought of his daughter Iphigeneia, whom he loved, who used to sing to him in his palace, and for whom he had wished to choose as husband one of the noblest of the Greeks. How could he, her father, find it in his heart to become her murderer? At first he refused to do the bidding of the prophet. In the end, however, as the ships remained motionless in harbour, as the army began to grow mutinous and as Calchas continued to claim the sacrifice due to the goddess, Agamemnon, against his better judgment, allowed himself to be persuaded.

He knew that his wife Clytemnestra would never allow their daughter to leave home with such a fate in store for her, and he sent a messenger to say that he wished Iphigeneia to come to Aulis not for the dreadful purpose which he planned but in order to become the wife of Achilles. So this wretched girl left the golden palace of Mycenae bringing with her the dresses and ornaments of a bride, little knowing that she was coming not to her wedding but to her death.

When her father met her in Aulis it was hard for him to hold back his tears. Instead of greeting her gladly, as she had expected him to do, he turned his head aside from her and covered his face in the folds of his royal cloak. Nor did she find Achilles there to be her husband. Achilles did not even know that his name had been used for the deception. As the priests approached her, it did not seem that they came as they might be coming to celebrate a wedding. There were no bridal songs, no gay dresses, no shouting for happiness. Instead she found herself taken up in the hands of men as though she were an animal and hurried to the altar. Here Calchas was waiting, and at first he concealed behind his back the cruel knife. In sudden terror Iphigeneia turned to her father, but again her father hid his face from her. She struggled and tried to run away, but the priests held her fast. They bent back the graceful head with its long tresses of carefully combed hair, as though it was the head of some goat or heifer that they were preparing to sacrifice. So in her youth and beauty, in her father's presence, at the very time when she should have been a bride, she was foully murdered, so that the fleet should have fair weather and prosperous winds.

This wicked deed, prompted by superstition, was to bring ruin in the end on Agamemnon himself. Now his wife Clytemnestra, whom he had left behind as queen in golden Mycenae, became his bitterest enemy. Soon after the sacrifice of Iphigeneia, the son of Thyestes, Aegisthus, came back to the plain of Argos. Clytemnestra welcomed him, secretly received his love and with him began to plot against the rightful king, her husband Agamemnon.

Meanwhile in Aulis it seemed that the sacrifice, cruel as it was, had at least satisfied the anger of the goddess. Fair winds began to blow and at last the great fleet was able to set out for Troy.

On their way there the Greeks cruelly deserted one of their number, and this act also was to cost them dear. It happened that the fleet put in to the island of Lemnos in order to find fresh water. Here the hero Philoctetes was bitten in the foot by a poisonous snake. No healing herbs or draughts could cure his wound which became worse and worse. Moreover the effect of the poison in the wound was to produce a terrible smell, so sickening that it was unpleasant to be anywhere near the wounded man. In the end the Greeks left Philoctetes behind in spite of his prayers to them that they would look after and help one of their own comrades. The Greeks who so shamefully deserted him little knew that it was fated that Troy could never be taken without the help of the bow and arrows of Herakles, the famous bow and arrows that had been given to Philoctetes when he, then only a boy, had lit the funeral pyre on which the hero died and from which he ascended to heaven to join the company of the gods. Now for many years Philoctetes remained, still suffering from his wound, deserted on the island of Lemnos. But he kept with him the great bow of Herakles and in the end the Greeks, in their need for him, repented of what they had done. Before that time many thousands on both sides had fallen in battle. Now the Greeks, ignorant of the troubles in front of them, set on for Troy and in Troy the Trojans and their allies prepared to resist the invaders.

VI

THE FIRST ACTIONS OF THE WAR

THE FLEET sailed on past islands, some of which are rocky and precipitous, waterless and uninhabited, while others are rich with vines and olives and herds of sheep and goats. On many of these islands grow all kinds of sweet smelling herbs, wild thyme, marjoram and many other flowers and shrubs. The warm wind would bring across the swelling waves the odour of these sweet herbs to those sailing still far from the shores where they grew. So sometimes the land could often be smelt before it could be seen. Yet it was not of these sweet and peaceful odours nor of the islands themselves that the Greeks thought as they pressed on in their black and painted ships to the destruction of the city of Troy.

It was at Sigeum that they made their landing. Beyond the long hills ran the rivers Scamander and Simois through the plain in which stood the huge walls of Troy with its wide streets, its towers and frowning battlements. But the Trojans were by no means content to await a siege behind their powerful fortifications. A Trojan army was drawn up on the beach ready to oppose the landing. As the Greek ships approached the shore the Greeks, staring out towards the flashing arms, the wheeling chariots and dense masses of their enemies, tried to distinguish among them the tall figures of the warriors of whom they had heard, the figures of Hector and of Aeneas and the other princes of Troy. Soon they had to raise their shields to cover them from the showers of arrows that met the approaching ships. But the helmsmen kept the ships straight on their course, and as ship after ship, with a grinding shock, ran upon the beach, so the warriors leapt out into the shallow water and began to fight their way inland through a storm of arrows and of spears.

They say that an oracle had revealed that the first of the Greeks to land on Trojan soil would certainly be killed. King Protesilaus either did not fear the oracle or else gallantly sacrificed himself for the good of his comrades. He had come to Troy leading an army from northern Greece and he had left behind him in his half-finished palace, a newly-married wife, Laodamia, whom he loved more than all else. Now his ship was the first to reach the shelving shore and he was the first to spring from the ship on to the land. He fell dead at once, struck through the gorgeous armour on his breast by the heavy ashen spear hurled at him by Hector. They say that when the news of his death reached his home, his loving wife Laodamia became distraught with grief. She had a wooden image made of her dead husband and kept it with her in her widowed bed. Her father wished to cure her of her excessive sorrow and he ordered the image to be burnt, hoping that afterwards his daughter would forget to mourn. But this was not at all what happened. Laodamia could not bear to be parted even from this wooden semblance of her love, and she threw herself into the flames in which the image was being consumed. Some say that then the gods had pity on Protesilaus and Laodamia, and that in another world they were permitted to enjoy their love.

Protesilaus, then, was the first to die at the hands of Hector and of the Trojans. Many others also on both sides perished before the Greeks were able to land upon the shore, to form themselves into battle order under their commanders and gradually to push the defenders backwards towards the hills and towards their city that lay beyond the hills.

By the end of the day's fighting the Greeks had established themselves firmly on Trojan soil. They began next to build a stockade around their ships to protect them from any raids that the enemy might make. Then, before advancing on Troy itself, they attacked the towns along the coast and inland which acknowledged the power of King Priam. These towns were well defended, and few if any of them yielded to the Greeks without hard fighting.

In all these battles along the coast Achilles with his Myrmidons distinguished himself above all others. When he led his men against the enemy, it seemed as though a raging fire was going through dry crops of corn. He took twelve towns along the coast and eleven inland, one of which was Lyrnessus in which lived the beautiful girl Briseis. Her father and her brothers had been killed by Achilles, but she, given to him as a slave in the division of the spoil, loved the fierce and brilliant hero tenderly, as he also loved her. She too was to be the cause of great trouble to the Greeks, but it was through no fault of her own that the trouble came.

Meanwhile, as Achilles ravaged the coast and plain, Hector led his armies out from Troy and wherever he went it seemed that he was as invincible as Achilles himself. Old Priam and the people of Troy looked on him as their great defender and their champion. As he set out day after day to battle, his loving wife Andromache and his little child, Astyanax, would look at him with proud and wondering eyes. Of all the Trojans he was not only the strongest, but the kindest also and the most honourable. Often Andromache would beg him to spare himself and in particular to avoid battle with Achilles; but in her heart she knew that Hector was fearless and that he would follow his duty wherever it might lead him. Yet now was not the time for these heroes to meet. Instead they looked for each other, like lions looking for their prey, and each, where he went, was unconquered. So therefore for nine years the Greeks and the Trojans fought at the outskirts of the city. Sometimes indeed the Trojans would be pressed inside their walls; but then again they would issue out again, and the fighting would be renewed between the river valleys of the Scamander and the Simois, so that, it seemed that neither would Troy ever be taken nor would the Greeks ever be driven back to their ships.

And as to the final issue of the conflict, the gods themselves were divided. Hera, the wife of Zeus, and Pallas Athene favoured the Greeks. Aphrodite, partly for the sake of Paris and partly for the sake of her own son Aeneas, was on the side of the Trojans. Ares, the god of War, who loved her, joined with her in this. So Zeus, the king of the gods, was perpetually pestered with the prayers and the complaints of his wife and of his children, some of whom urged him to give his help to Hector and his armies so that the Greeks might be driven into the sea, while others demanded that he should support Agamemnon and Achilles and allow them at last to sack the proud citadel of Troy. As it was Zeus gave his aid now to one side, now to another; for the time had not yet come for the decision to be taken. Before that time came it was necessary for many more of the Greeks and of the Trojans to lose their lives in this lamentable war. Indeed it was after nine years of fighting that the greatest slaughter of all took place because of the quarrel, so destructive to all, between Achilles and King Agamemnon.

BOOK TWO

THE WRATH OF ACHILLES

I

THE GREAT QUARREL

THE REASON for the quarrel between Agamemnon and Achilles was, in the first place, the god Apollo who sent a plague upon the army because Agamemnon had treated Chryses, Apollo's own priest, with discourtesy.

What happened was this. The Greeks had sacked the city where Chryses lived and made prisoners of its inhabitants. Among the prisoners was the young daughter of the priest and she, in the division of the plunder, was given to Agamemnon for his own.

Now old Chryses, in sorrow for the loss of his daughter, came to the Greek camp, bringing a full ransom and carrying in his hand a golden staff and the sacred crown that he wore as priest of Apollo. He spoke to all the Greeks, but particularly to the sons of Atreus, Agamemnon and Menelaus. "Great sons of Atreus," he said, "and all you other Greeks, may the gods who dwell in Olympus grant you your desire in taking the great city of Priam. But first, I beg you, show your reverence for Apollo, the Archer God; receive this ample ransom, and give me back my daughter."

The army applauded the words of the priest and would gladly have accepted his rich gifts and given back the girl to him. Agamemnon however thought differently. He spoke rudely to the priest and said, "Old man, don't let me find you any longer today about our hollow ships, or coming back here again another time. If I do, your golden staff and your crown will not preserve your life. So far from

32

giving you back your daughter, I intend that she shall grow old in my house in Mycenae, far from her own country. Now be off with you! Do not make me angry, if you want to get back alive."

Trembling with fear the old man obeyed him. But when he came to the shore of the breaking sea he stretched out his hands and prayed to his master Apollo. "O hear me," he cried, "God of the silver bow! Reward me now for the temples I have built for you and for the fat thighs of oxen that I have sacrificed at your altars. By your weapons let the Greeks suffer for my tears!"

Apollo heard his prayer and came down in anger from the high peaks of Olympus. His bow was in his hand and the arrows clanged in the quiver at his back. He came like night falls, and very soon his presence was felt beside the ships of the Greeks. First he turned his anger against the animals —mules and dogs; but before long men too fell before his arrows. Man after man fell dead and by day and night countless fires were burning to consume the dead bodies.

So for nine days the Greeks suffered at the hands of Apollo, and then Hera, fearing that the whole army would be destroyed or be forced to sail home with Troy un-conquered, put it into the heart of Achilles to call a council of the Kings and chieftains. When the council was assembled Achilles spoke first to their leader, Agamemnon. "King Agamemnon," he said, "so many of us now have died in the fighting and by the plague, that before long I fear we shall have to return home with our task uncompleted. Could we not therefore consult some prophet or oracle who could tell us why the gods are angry with us? Perhaps Apollo will accept some sacrifice, and so the army can be saved."

Then the prophet Calchas rose to his feet. "Lord Achilles," he said, "before I say what I wish to say, will you swear to protect me? There may be great men who will not like my words, and I dare not speak them unless I am sure that you will stand by me."

"Speak on," replied Achilles. "So long as I am alive, not one of the Greeks shall touch a hair of your head, not Agamemnon himself, if it is he that you fear."

This promise gave Calchas confidence. "Apollo is angry with us," he said, "because King Agamemnon has dishonoured his priest and refuses to give back his daughter, even though full ransom was offered for her. His anger will never cease until the old man's daughter is restored to him, and offerings are made by the army to Apollo's temple."

Now Agamemnon sprang to his feet. His heart was heavy with anger and his eyes blazed like fire. "As for you, Calchas," he said, "you have never once prophesied anything good. Always you have something evil to say, as on this present occasion when you claim that the gods blame me for keeping the bright-eyed daughter of Chryses. Indeed I had no wish to accept a ransom for her. I prefer her to my own wife Clytemnestra, whom she excels in beauty and intelligence and in all the works that women do. Nevertheless I will return her to her father, since I consider the safety of the army more important than my own desires. But you others must see to it that I am given a proper compensation for what I lose. It is hardly right that I should be the only one of the Greeks without a proper share in what we have won."

Achilles immediately replied to him. "Your avarice," he said, "goes beyond all bounds. How do you imagine that we are going to find you a special prize? All the spoils of war have already been divided and we cannot start dividing them all over again. No, give the girl back to her father and, if ever the Gods allow us to capture the great walls of Troy, we will pay you back three or four times the value of what you have lost."

Agamemnon looked at him in bitterness and anger. "Achilles," he said, "you may be a good soldier, and like the gods in battle, but you cannot trick me like this. It is I who am King here and Commander in Chief of the army.

These are my terms. Find me something of equal value to what I am giving up, and I will say no more about it. If you do not, I shall take what I want for myself. Yes, I shall send my men to you or to Ajax or to Odysseus and I shall make away with one or other of the prizes that you have won in battle. This I shall certainly do, unless I am satisfied. I give you fair warning of it. And now let a ship be launched and let some responsible general, Ajax or Odysseus or Idomeneus, take the girl and take offerings with her and bring her back to her father, so that Apollo may look kindly on us."

Now the mind of Achilles was on fire with anger and again he leapt to his feet. "Have you absolutely no sense of shame?" he said. "Do you never think of anything but your own profit? How can you expect any of us to go on fighting for your sake? As for me, the Trojans never did me any harm, never robbed my herds or made war upon my men. Between their land and mine is a whole echoing sea and chain after chain of shadowy mountains. It was for your sake, you dog, and for the sake of Menelaus that I came here and have been in the front of the fighting ever since. And now you actually dare to threaten to take away the prize of war that the soldiers gave me. Yet in fact, when the plunder is shared out, it is always you who get the most. That is what you are good at, making yourself rich at the expense of other men's lives. When it comes to fighting it is I who bear the full brunt of it, and in the end am rewarded poorly for doing most. Why should I stay here to make you rich? Why do I not sail home again and become happy in my own country?"

Agamemnon looked at him with bitter hatred. "There is nothing to prevent you running away," he said, "if that is what you want to do. There are plenty of others here who respect me as they ought, and we can quite well do without you. I admit that you are a great soldier. But it was the gods who made you strong, and there is no need for you to claim all the credit for yourself. As it is you love nothing in the world but violence and fighting. Go home now with your ships and your Myrmidons. I am not frightened by your temper. But let me tell you this: just as Apollo is taking my prize from me, so I shall send to your tents and take from you the girl Briseis, who is your prize. So you will learn that I am stronger than you and in future others will not dare, as you have done, to oppose my will."

Now a great pain came over Achilles. His heart bounded within his shaggy breast, and he was in two minds, whether to draw his huge sword from his thigh, cut his way through the others and kill Agamemnon, or whether to curb his mounting anger. Already he was beginning to draw his sword when the goddess Athene, the daughter of Zeus, came down to him from heaven and stood at his side, invisible to all the rest, but visible to Achilles, who recognised the goddess and said to her, "Why have you come to me, daughter of Zeus? Is it to see how I am insulted by Agamemnon? I tell you that this arrogance of his is going to cost him his life."

The grey-eyed goddess Athene answered him: "Remember," she said, "that I and the goddess Hera love you. You must take our advice. Be angry in words, if you will; but do not draw your sword. I tell you for certain that a time will come when Agamemnon will have such need of you that he will offer you three or four times the gifts and the prizes which now are in dispute."

Reluctantly Achilles thrust the huge sword back into its sheath. "It is right," he said, "to obey the gods, and the gods listen to those who obey them." Then Athene sped back to the company of the gods in Olympus, and Achilles turned again on Agamemnon. "You drunken brute," he said, "who look like a dog and fight like a trembling doe, you who never have enough courage to join in an ambush or fight in the front ranks, since it pays you better to steal what belongs to others, now listen to the oath that I swear. I swear by the kingly sceptre that I hold in my hands that the day will come when you will all yearn to have me at your side, when thousands of the Greeks will be falling before the spear of man-slaughtering Hector, when you will be powerless to prevent the slaughter and when your heart will know all the bitterness of remorse for having treated dishonourably the best man among the Greeks."

When he had spoken, he hurled to the ground his sceptre which was studded with golden studs, and he sat down in his place.

Now Nestor, the old King of Pylos, old enough indeed to have been the grandfather of either Agamemnon or Achilles, rose to his feet and tried, though vainly enough, to heal the quarrel. "Alas! Alas!" he said, "What a terrible thing is happening to all the land of Greece! How delighted Priam and his sons would be, if they could see you two, the greatest of the Greeks, at variance with each other! Will you not listen to my words, the words of an old man who has known in the past great heroes like Theseus of Athens and Pirithous, his friend. Yet these great men used to listen to me and be persuaded by what I said. Agamemnon, do not take from Achilles the prize that was given him by the army. Do not insult the best of your soldiers. And, Achilles, though you are so great a warrior, you ought to show more respect to our Commander in Chief, one who rules over more men than you do. Kings have their authority from Zeus. Do you not see, both of you, that you are wrong? Only the Trojans can benefit from this quarrel."

"Nestor, my old friend," said Agamemnon, "what you say is, as usual, full of sense. But this man has no respect for authority. He wishes to be supreme. I am not going to be governed by him. Certainly the gods made him a good spearsman, but that gives him no right to insult kings."

At this point Achilles interrupted him. "And what a fool and coward," he said, "I should be thought, if I always and in every way gave in to you! You can order others about but not me any more. And here is another thing. As for the girl Briseis, the army gave her to me, and I shall not resist you if you take her away. But you cannot touch anything else of mine by my black ship. Come and try, so that the rest may see the result. I tell you that soon enough your blood would be pouring black about the blade of my spear."

With these words Achilles rose from the council. Patroclus, his friend, and all his men followed him, all resolved not to engage again in the war until their leader ordered them.

Then, at the command of Agamemnon, the wise Odysseus took the daughter of the priest Chryses in a swift ship back again to her father. He brought gifts with him and the proper offerings for the Archer god Apollo. The old man was pleased to see his daughter safe and sound, pleased too with the gifts and the offerings. Once more he prayed to Apollo, begging him now to spare the Greeks from the pestilence which was destroying them. And once more Apollo listened to his prayer. No longer did the funeral pyres burn for the dead in the Greek camp. Yet, though they were spared from the anger of the god, many more, because of the quarrel between Achilles and Agamemnon, would soon fall before the spears of Hector and the Trojans.

Agamemnon was far from forgetting the quarrel. He called for his two heralds, Talthybius and Eurybates, and told them to go to Achilles' tent and bring back with them the girl Briseis. "If he will not give her up to you," he said, "tell him that I shall come myself in full force to take her."

Trembling and abashed, the two heralds came to the camp of the Myrmidons, scarcely daring to address their words to Achilles. But Achilles received them courteously. "Heralds," he said, "you are welcome. My quarrel is not with you, but with Agamemnon who sent you. Only I ask you to remember this day on the day when Agamemnon will need me most and, with all his forces, will not keep Hector from driving him to his ships." Then he asked his friend Patroclus to bring out the lady Briseis and to give her into the keeping of the two heralds. Patroclus obeyed him and the girl was led away weeping.

II

ACHILLES AND HIS MOTHER

THEN ACHILLES, in the pain of his heart, went by himself, leaving his companions behind him, to the shore of the grey sea. Here he sat down, looking out over the boundless deep, and, stretching out his hands, he prayed to his mother Thetis. "Mother," he said, "you it was who gave me life, but my life is destined to be only a short one. Since this is so Zeus ought at least to have given me honour. Yet now I am insulted by King Agamemnon."

As he spoke, the tears fell from his eyes. But his mother heard him from where she was sitting in the depths of the sea beside her old father Nereus, the sea god. She rose quickly, like a mist, through the grey salt water and came to her son, laying her hand gently on his arm. "My son," she said, "why are you weeping? Tell me, so that both of us may know."

Achilles groaned as he answered her. "Mother," he said, "you are a goddess and you know everything." Yet he told her the whole story of the quarrel, and at the end he begged her to go to Zeus himself, to clasp his knees and beg him to bring sorrow on the Greeks, to give aid to the Trojans so that Hector might drive the army of Agamemnon back to their ships and that Agamemnon might repent of his treatment of the best of all his warriors.

"My child," said Thetis, when he had finished, "indeed I have suffered in giving birth to you. I wish that you could sit here by your ships without tears and without any

39

sorrow, since your fate is so brief, lasting for so short a time. As it is your life is not only shorter than that of others, but also more full of pain. Now indeed I will go to the snowy summit of Olympus and will speak to Zeus, the Thunderer, as you ask me to do, though yesterday he went with all the rest of the blessed gods to the stream of Ocean to join in a banquet with the blameless Ethiopians. But in twelve days he will return to Olympus, and then I shall speak to him. Meanwhile, you must preserve your anger and hold back from the fighting."

So Achilles stayed by his ships. Neither he nor Patroclus nor any of the Myrmidons took part in the war. Instead they spent their time in racing, in throwing the javelin or the discus, in singing and in feasting.

And after twelve days Zeus with the other gods returned to Olympus. Then Thetis rose out of the waves of the sea, ascended into the sky and found the Father of Gods and men seated apart from the others on the highest peak of the heavenly mountain. Thetis sank down at his feet. With her left arm she clasped his knees and, like a suppliant, she touched his chin with her right hand. "Father Zeus," she implored him, "if I have ever done you any good service now grant me my prayers and give honour to my son, who was born to have a shorter fate than most men. Now, as you know, King Agamemnon has dishonoured him by taking from him his prize. Avenge him, I beg you, and give your aid to the Trojans so that the Greeks may reverence Achilles and pay him the honour that is his due."

Zeus did not answer her at once. For a long time he sat still in silence, with Thetis clinging to his knees. Finally she spoke again. "Just nod your head," she said, "to show that you have granted my prayer. Or, if you will, refuse me. Then I shall know that with you I am given less consideration than any other one of the gods."

Zeus sighed and said, "Indeed you are causing me great embarrassment. This is certain to lead to more quarrels

between me and Hera, my wife, who even now is constantly
complaining that I favour the Trojans too much. You had
better leave me now, or she is sure to notice what is happening. But to show you that I will grant your prayer, I will nod
my head. This is a promise that can never be broken, and
as I say so certainly shall I do."

Then Zeus bowed his head and, as he did so, the dark
ambrosial hair swung forward and all Olympus shook.

So Thetis darted down from shining Olympus into the
depths of the sea, and Zeus went to his own palace. As he
entered it all the gods rose from their chairs to show their
respect for their father. Zeus sat down on his throne, but
Hera guessed immediately that some plot had been made
between him and the silver-footed goddess Thetis. At once
she turned on him and said: "I know that some goddess
has been scheming with you. This is what you always do.
As soon as I am not there, you begin to decide things
secretly behind my back. You never really take me into your
confidence and tell me what you are going to do."

Zeus answered her and said, "Hera, you must not expect
to know everything that passes in my mind. You could not
bear the knowledge, even though you are my wife. I tell
you first before all the others, when I have something which
is fitting to be told. But when I reach a private decision of
my own, it is not for you to question me about it."

Hera looked at him with her large eyes, like the eyes of
oxen. "Great son of Kronos," she said, "I cannot imagine
what you mean. Have I ever asked you questions about
your private decisions or tried to interfere with you in any
way? All the same I am terribly afraid that silver-footed
Thetis has been using her arts on you and has persuaded
you to help the Trojans in order to bring glory to Achilles."

"As for you," Zeus replied, "you are always leaping to
conclusions. Perhaps you are right. If so, then this is my
will. There is nothing you can do about it. I advise you to
sit quietly in your place and to submit. For if I once was

driven to lay my hands on you, not all the gods in Olympus could protect you."

At these words the ox-eyed Hera trembled and was afraid. She said no more, but sat in silence, though in her heart she was angry enough. Among all the gods there was silence, until the lame Hephaestus, the god of fire, spoke and said: "This is a sad business, if you two are going to quarrel simply for the sake of mortals. How can we enjoy our good food and drink, if our minds are on these other inferior things? I would recommend my mother to make peace with our father Zeus, or he may grow more angry still and then our dinner would be ruined. He might even hurl his thunderbolts at us, and then where would we be? No, mother, I beg you to ask his parden, and then he will look kindly on us again."

As he spoke he carried to Hera a great cup filled with nectar, the wine of the gods, and urged her to drink and forget her anger. Then he began to serve all the other gods, beginning from the left, mixing their drinks for them in a golden mixing bowl. As they watched him bustling about in the banqueting hall, unquenchable laughter arose among the blessed gods. They sat cheerfully together, in no lack of food or drink or of the sweet music of the lyre, which Apollo played, while the Muses sang to his accompaniment. And when the bright light of the sun had set they departed each one to his own palace, palaces built for them by the cunning craftsman Hephaestus. Zeus himself lay down in the upper chamber where he was accustomed to sleep, and Hera lay beside him.

III

THE FALSE DREAM

S O SLEEP came to the gods and to the warriors before
Troy, to all except to Zeus. He stayed awake, pondering
how he could avenge Achilles and have the Greeks
slaughtered by their ships. What seemed to him the best
plan was to send a false dream to Agamemnon. So he
called to him one of the shadowy dreams that live in the
house of Sleep, and when the dream came to him, he said:
"False dream, go to the Greek ships and to the tent of
Agamemnon. Say to him that now is the time for his soldiers
to put on their armour and go into battle. Say that the
immortal gods are now all of one mind. Hera's prayers
have persuaded the rest. Doom is descending upon the
Trojans and now he will be able to capture the city with its
broad streets."

So he spoke, and the dream, going down to the ships,
found Agamemnon sleeping in his tent. The dream stood at his
head and put on the shape of the old counsellor Nestor, whom
Agamemnon honoured most, and spoke to the sleeping
King: "Are you asleep, great son of Atreus? This is no time
for sleep, and certainly not for you, who have so many cares
upon your mind. Now listen to me. I come as a messenger
from Zeus who, though he is far from you, still watches
over you and pities you. He bids me to tell you to make
ready your forces at once for battle. Now the immortal gods
are all of one mind. Hera's prayers have persuaded the rest.
Doom is descending upon the Trojans and now you will be

able to capture the city with its broad streets. Remember
my words and keep them firmly in your mind when you
wake from sleep."

So the dream slipped away and left Agamemnon with
thoughts in his mind that were not going to come true. For
he thought that he would take Priam's city that very day,
little knowing what would really happen and that Zeus
intended first to lay countless more sufferings both on the
Trojans and on the Greeks in the hard and stubborn
fighting. When he woke up, the divine voice was still
ringing in his ears. He sat up on his bed, put on his soft
tunic, and then threw his heavy cloak over his shoulders.
He bound the bright sandals on his feet, slung round his
neck his great sword with its silver-studded sheath, and
took in his hand the royal sceptre of the house of Atreus.
Then, as dawn was just beginning to show, he went out of
his tent and walked among the Greek ships. First he came
to the camp of Nestor and here, by Nestor's ship, he summoned a council of the chief leaders of the army—Ajax
and Idomeneus, Menelaus, Diomedes and Odysseus. When
he had told them of his dream Nestor spoke first
and said: "If this dream had come to anyone else, we might
have doubted it and thought it false. But as it is, it has come
to King Agamemnon, our Commander-in-chief. I say
therefore that we should at once call an assembly of the
whole army and then lead out all our forces to battle in the
plain before Troy."

The others approved of the old man's advice, and heralds
went about the camp calling the soldiers to the assembly.
They came together in their vast numbers to the meeting
place, so many of them that it took nine heralds, all shouting
at the tops of their voices, to make the troops settle quietly
in their places and listen to the words of their commander.
Now all of them were mustered except for the Myrmidons,
the followers of Achilles. They, with their great leader,
remained in their camp. Agamemnon spoke to them and

said: "Soldiers of the Greeks, the time has come for our final attack on Troy. The first thing to do is for us all to have a meal, so that we may be fit for a day of battle. Sharpen your spears, see to it that your shields are properly fitted. Feed your swift horses well and make your chariots ready for action. We shall fight throughout the whole day, with no pause and no letting up in the fighting until night comes. The straps of your shields will stick to your breasts in the heat of battle; hands will weary on the spear shafts; horses will be soaked with sweat as they pull the polished chariots. Let me find no one hanging back from the war or cowering by the ships. If I do, he shall lie where I find him and be meat for the vultures and for the dogs."

When he had finished speaking, the army roared out its applause with a noise like the roar of the sea breaking in storm upon a rocky coast. They left the assembly to prepare their meal, to look over their equipment and to make ready for the great battle. Each man made offerings to the god whom he honoured most, praying that he might still be alive when the sun set. Agamemnon himself sacrificed a fat five year old ox to almighty Zeus and he invited the leaders of the Greeks to share in the feast. As the animal was being sacrificed Agamemnon prayed: "O great and powerful Zeus, God of the black clouds and dweller in heaven, I pray that before the sun sets in darkness I may bring down in flames the high palace of Priam, that my spear may rip through the brazen armour that covers Hector's breast, and that his friends and companions at his side may roll dying on the ground and bite the dust."

So he prayed, but Zeus did not grant his prayer. He received the sacrifice indeed, but in return he was planning death and destruction for the Greeks.

Now when the feast and the sacrifices were over, the captains and commanders led their men into the plain. They streamed out in innumerable hordes, like the flocks of birds—cranes or geese or long-necked swans—that can be seen along the rivers of Asia, filling all the meadows with their cries and the flapping of their wings as they wheel and turn about. But soon the officers had brought their men into battle order. Company stood by company in correct formation, and Agamemnon went along the ranks, urging on the troops to war. Then the whole army moved forward over the plain, and as they moved the dust rose into the air and the very earth shook beneath the tramping of their feet.

Meanwhile in Troy, Hector and the Trojan leaders were in the palace of Priam, discussing the conduct of the war. To them Zeus sent his own messenger Iris, goddess of the rainbow. She came in the appearance of one of the Trojan sentries who had been posted far out on the plain to watch for any signs of movement in the Greek camp. Standing before King Priam she said: "My Lord, this is no time for talking as one might do in peace time. Now the full flood of war is loosed upon us. I have been in many battles, but I have never seen a force to compare with the one that is now coming towards us over the plain to fight at our gates. Now, Hector, is the time to meet them with every single man of us who can bear arms."

Hector immediately recognised the voice of the goddess. He dismissed the meeting and gave the call to arms. The gates of the city were flung wide open and into the plain poured the armies of the Trojans and their allies, infantry, cavalry and chariots.

IV

THE DUEL

S O THE two armies approached each other, the Trojans
with a noise of shouting and the clashing of arms, the
Greeks in a grim silence. Above them eddied the clouds
of dust raised by their marching feet and the feet of their
swift horses. Each side was bent on war, each side determined not to yield.

And now, when the armies were close to each other and
on the point of joining battle, Paris stepped forward from
the Trojan ranks, ready to challenge any Greek champion
to fight in single combat. Over his armour he wore a
panther's skin; his curved bow and sword were slung from
his shoulders, and in his hands he held two sharp spears of
bronze.

Menelaus saw him and when he saw that it was Paris
striding out in front of the army, offering battle to the
Greeks, he felt as glad as a hungry lion feels when he comes
upon the body of a stag or a wild goat in the mountains. So,
seeing Paris before his eyes, he felt sure of his revenge on the
man who had wronged him. With all his armour he sprang down
from his chariot and made his way through the first ranks.

But when Paris saw Menelaus coming forward to meet
him, he turned pale and took a step backwards, like someone
who has suddenly seen a snake on the ground in some
wooded glade and who starts backward in terror. So Paris
felt his limbs tremble, and he made his way hurriedly back
again behind the cover of the ranks of Trojans.

Hector saw him as he shrank back, and shouted out to him with bitter words: "You wretched Paris, you who are so good to look at, you who are so mad about women, you traitor! I wish you had never been born or had died before you found a wife. That would have been better than for you to bring shame on us all. Certainly the long-haired Greeks will laugh when they see us putting you forward as our champion, when you have nothing but your good looks to recommend you, no courage, no steadfastness. You took the wife of Menelaus and now you dare not stand up to him in battle. If you did, all your lyre-playing would not help you, nor would your good looks nor your curled hair nor all the gifts that Aphrodite has given you. You would soon be lying in the dust. But we Trojans are too considerate. Otherwise you would have been stoned to death long ago for all the trouble you have given us."

Paris replied to his brother. "Hector," he said, "what you say is right and I cannot complain about it. You have a spirit that is always resolute and energetic. It is like an axe cutting through wood. But you ought not to mock at the beautiful gifts of Aphrodite. The gifts of the gods should not be despised, even though one might have preferred to have had other gifts instead. And now I will do as you wish and fight with Menelaus. Let the others lay down their arms and let Menelaus and me fight in the space between the armies. Let us agree that whoever wins shall keep Helen and all her possessions. Then there can be a treaty of peace, so that the Trojans can live happily in Troy and the Greeks can return to their own land."

Hector was delighted with this proposal. He pushed back the front ranks of the Trojans and ordered them to sit down on the ground. Then he stepped forward towards the Greek army who still hurled javelins at him and shot arrows which rang upon his shield and upon his armour. But Agamemnon shouted out to his men to stop shooting. "Great Hector," he said, "has some proposal which

he wishes to make to us.   Let us listen to what he has
to say."

So Hector spoke to the Greek army and told them of the
offer that Paris had made. Menelaus replied to him. "One
of us," he said, "must die, and it is good for the rest of you,
who have suffered enough already through the quarrel
between me and Paris, to make peace. But I do not trust the
sons of Priam. Let Priam himself come and let us sacrifice
to Zeus and to the Earth and to the Sun, and let both sides
swear on oath that the winner of this battle shall keep Helen
and her possessions, and that afterwards there shall be peace."

Both Greeks and Trojans were pleased with the words of
Menelaus. Both sides longed for there to be an end to the
bitter fighting, and now it seemed that, whatever the result
of the battle, peace would be assured. But this was by no
means the will of Zeus, who was determined that the
fighting should become more furious still and more bitter
than ever it had been.

Now the soldiers laid down their arms, unyoked the horses
from the chariots, and prepared to watch the duel. Hector
sent heralds back to the town of Troy to inform Priam of
what had passed and to bring the animals for the sacrifice.

Yet before the heralds reached the city Helen herself had
heard the news. Iris, the messenger of the Gods, came
down to her from heaven, having put on the appearance of
her sister-in-law, one of the beautiful daughters of Priam.
She came to Helen in her rich palace and found her weaving
a great purple web on which were shown the battles fought
for her sake between the Trojans and the Greeks. Iris said
to her "Come with me, dear sister, and see what is happening
in the plain. Just now the two armies were about to join
together in battle; but now they are standing quietly in their
places. The men are leaning on their shields and their
spears are stuck into the ground at their sides. Paris and
great Menelaus are going to fight together in single combat,
and the winner is to take you for his wife."

As she spoke, Helen felt in her heart the sweetness of a longing for her former husband and for her native land and for her parents. She put a white veil on her head. and with tears in her eyes she left the gorgeous bedchamber and, accompanied by two waiting women, went out to the gate that overlooked the armies in the plain. It was the gate called the Scaean Gate and here on the tower above the gate were sitting Priam and the old counsellors of Troy. These men were now too old for battle; their fighting days were over; but they were still excellent in debate, good talkers and enjoying their talk as they sat there together, like grasshoppers chirping together melodiously in the sunny grass. When they saw Helen walking to the tower, they raised their eyes, and one would say to another: "No wonder that Greeks and Trojans have suffered so long for such a woman! Her face is like the face of the immortal gods. Yet all the same, and in spite of her loveliness, it would be better for her to sail away in her ships and not bring trouble on us and on our children."

Priam also saw her and called her to him. "Come here, my dear child," he said, "and sit by me, so that you can see your former husband and your friends and relations among the Greeks. I have never blamed you. No, it is the gods who are to blame for fastening upon us all the grievous load of this terrible war. Now tell me who is that huge man over there who towers head and shoulders above the rest. I don't think that I have ever seen anyone so fine looking or with such an air of authority. His bearing is the bearing of a king."

Helen answered him and said: "O my dear father-in-law, I both love and respect you. How I wish that I had died before I came here with your son and became the cause of so much trouble to you, leaving my own home and my little daughter and all my dear friends. But I had to do it, and now my heart is full of pain. Now I will answer your question. The man you see there is Agamemnon, the son of Atreus, a great King and good with the spear. Once he was my brother-in-law, disgraceful creature that I am—unless all that part of my life was a dream."

"So that is Agamemnon," said Priam, "the fortunate man, favoured by the gods and ruler over so vast a host. Now who is that other one near by? He is a head shorter than Agamemnon, but broader in the shoulders and chest. His armour is lying on the ground, and he himself is going the rounds of his troops. He looks like a great ram marshalling a herd of white sheep."

"That," said Helen, "is Odysseus, the son of Laertes, who comes from the rocky island of Ithaca. There is no one like him for wisdom and cunning and resourcefulness."

Here one of Priam's counsellors, the wise Antenor, joined the conversation. "I remember him well," he said. "Both he and Menelaus once came here on an embassy and I entertained them in my house. When we were standing up, Menelaus stood a head taller than all the rest; but when we were sitting down, Odysseus seemed the bigger man. They were quite different too in their style of speaking. Menelaus is a man of few words; he speaks simply and directly and makes his meaning plain. But when Odysseus got up to speak, he first of all looked all round him from under his shaggy eyebrows; he made no gestures with the sceptre that he carried, but held it stiffly. Indeed he looked as though he had never made a speech before. But then suddenly his great voice came from his chest; the words whirled about us like winter snowflakes; his eyes flashed. At such moments no one could possibly compete with him, and we wondered at him as we listened spell-bound."

Then Priam enquired from Helen the names of other leaders of the Greeks and she pointed out to him the mighty Ajax, Diomedes, Idomeneus and others. She looked in vain for her two brothers, Castor and Polydeuces. "Perhaps," she thought, "they would not join the army, because they feared reproaches for their sister's shame." She did not know that they were already buried in the earth of Sparta, in their own dear native land.

But now the heralds from the army came to King Priam to deliver their message. "Hector and Agamemnon," they said, "are calling for your presence at a solemn sacrifice. Paris and Menelaus are to fight together for Helen. The winner is to keep her and all her possessions; and after the battle we are to make peace, so that we may live undisturbed in Troy, and the Greeks will return to their own land."

Priam sighed as he heard the news, since, though he longed for peace, he feared for the life of his son. Quickly his horses were yoked to his shining chariot and he set out through the Scaean Gate towards the armies. He passed through the Trojan ranks and approached the Greeks. Agamemnon and Odysseus rose to greet him and in the space between the armies the animals were prepared for sacrifice.

When the sacrifices were made to Zeus, to the Sun, to the Earth and to the Powers under the earth, the kings called the gods to witness their solemn oaths. Each man in the armies, both Trojans and Greeks, prayed also. "Almighty Zeus," they prayed, "and you other immortal gods, if either side breaks this treaty, we pray that their brains may be poured out on the ground like wine, and the brains of their children too, and that their wives may pass into the hands of strangers."

So they prayed for peace, but Zeus did not intend to answer their prayers.

Then Priam spoke: "I myself," he said, "am going back to the towers of Troy. I cannot bear to watch while my dear son fights with great Menelaus. But I think that Zeus knows already which of the two is fated to die."

So Priam, and Antenor with him, mounted their chariot and drove back to the city.

Meanwhile Hector and Odysseus were measuring out the ground where the contest would take place. Then they put two pebbles in a bronze helmet, one for Paris and one for Menelaus. This was to decide which of the two should have the first throw with his spear. Next Hector took the helmet and, turning his head aside, shook it to and fro. The pebble that first leapt out was the one that had the mark of Paris on it.

Then Paris began to put on his beautiful armour. Round his legs he tied the splendid greaves with silver fastenings on the ankles. Next he put on his breastplate; it was one that he had borrowed from his brother Lycaon. Over his shoulders he slung a bronze sword with silver studs on the hilt, and then a great shield of toughened ox-hide. On his head he put a helmet with a nodding horse-hair crest, and then in his strong hands he grasped a heavy spear.

Menelaus armed himself in the same way, and now the two champions strode out from behind the ranks of their own men and stood facing each other on the measured ground. First Paris hurled his long-shadowed spear. It landed full upon the shield of Menelaus, but did not break through. The point bent on the strong shield.

Now Menelaus poised his spear in his hands and, as he did so, he prayed to Father Zeus. "King Zeus," he said, "give me my revenge on Paris who was the first to injure me. Let him fall before my hand, so that in the future men may tremble at his fate and may shrink from doing harm to their hosts who have welcomed them kindly!"

So saying, he hurled his spear with such force that it pierced right through Paris's shield and through his breastplate. But Paris swerved aside and avoided death. The point of the spear tore the tunic on his skin and just grazed his flesh. Then Menelaus drew his sword and, leaping forward, brought it down with his full strength on his enemy's gleaming helmet. Paris was half stunned, but the sword, as it struck, broke into pieces and fell from Menelaus's hand. Menelaus groaned aloud and turned his eyes to heaven. "O Father Zeus," he said, "you are the most ungracious of the gods. Truly I thought that I had revenged myself on Paris for the wrong he did me; but now my sword is broken in my hands and I scarcely touched him with my spear."

And now, before Paris could recover himself, Menelaus sprang at him again and seized him by the great crest upon his helmet. Then he began to drag him backwards towards the Greek lines. The strap of the helmet pressed into Paris's tender throat and he himself was half strangled. Indeed Menelaus was on the point of dragging him off the ground and of winning all the glory of the victory. But Aphrodite, the goddess, saw what was happening to her favourite. It was she who caused the helmet strap to break, although it was made of stout ox-hide. So Menelaus was left with the empty helmet in his strong hand. He threw it behind him into the ranks of his own men, who took it up and kept it for him as a trophy. Then he rushed upon Paris again, longing to make an end of him with his spear. But Aphrodite easily, as gods are able to, saved him. She threw a thick mist around him and, while Menelaus searched for his enemy in the mist, she took Paris up and set him down on his soft bed in his own perfumed bedroom in Troy.

There Helen found him. She turned her eyes away from him and said: "So you have returned. I wish you had fallen at the hands of the great warrior who used to be my husband. You used to boast that you were a better man than he is, stronger in the arm and more skilful in the use of your weapons. Why then do you not challenge him again? But I should advise you not to. You would certainly be destroyed."

"Do not blame me, my dear wife," said Paris. "Menelaus has won on this occasion. It was the goddess Athene who helped him. Another time I shall win. I have gods to help me too. But now let us enjoy our love together. I confess that I have never felt so fond of you and so deeply in love as I do now, not even at the time when I first took you from Sparta on my swift ship and we stopped together for the night on the island of Cranae."

Meanwhile as they talked together in their bedroom, Menelaus was going about like a wild beast searching for his prey. He looked for Paris everywhere in the Greek and Trojan ranks but nowhere could he find him, nor could anyone point him out. No one indeed would have hidden him out of kindness. They all hated him like black death.

Finally Agamemnon spoke. "Trojans and allies of Troy," he said, "it is plain that Menelaus is the conqueror. Now it is for you to fulfil your part of the bargain and to give us back Helen with all her wealth."

As he spoke all the Greek army applauded him.

V

THE TRUCE IS BROKEN

MEANWHILE THE gods were sitting in their heavenly palace, drinking nectar out of golden cups and looking down upon what was happening in the plain of Troy. Zeus indeed had no intention of allowing the fighting to stop, but now he spoke in order to irritate his wife Hera. "I know," he said, "that there are two goddesses, Hera and Athene, who are on the side of the Greeks. Yet they seem merely to be sitting here and looking on while the laughter-loving Aphrodite has shown herself most energetic in supporting her side. Only just now she has rescued Paris from the hands of that great warrior Menelaus. Still it is quite evident that Menelaus has won the battle, and now the city of Priam will be preserved and the Greeks will return home with Helen."

The words of Zeus made both Hera and Athene angry. They were determined that Troy should be utterly destroyed. Athene controlled her anger, but Hera could not do so. "Great Zeus," she said, "you surprise me. Do you wish me to have had all my trouble for nothing. Both I and my horses were covered with sweat at the time I went all over Greece summoning the great leaders to the war. And now is Troy to escape? You may do as you like, but certainly not all of us will approve of it."

Zeus spoke sharply to her. "What harm," he said, "have Priam and his sons done to you? Why should you be so determined to destroy their beautiful city? For my part I love old Priam and his people. He has always sacrificed to me as he should do, and in all the world Troy is the city that I love best."

"The cities that I love best," said Hera, "are Argos and Sparta and golden Mycenae. Destroy any one of these, if you will. I shall not stand against you. Yet I deserve some consideration too, since I am your wife. All I ask now is that you should allow Athene to go down to the battlefield and contrive matters so that the Trojans will break the truce."

This in fact was what Zeus wished to do and so he readily gave his permission to his child, grey-eyed Athene. She sped down to earth like a shooting star, and as the men on the plain saw the flash in the sky that marked her coming, they gazed at each other with wide eyes and they said: "What does this mean? Does it mean that Zeus is giving us peace, or is it war again and all the miseries of war?"

Meanwhile Athene had put on the appearance of a Trojan warrior and was searching through the Trojan ranks for the famous archer Pandarus. She found him standing among the spearmen whom he commanded and, taking him aside, she said: "Pandarus, why not win fame and gratitude from all the Trojans, and especially from Paris? There is Menelaus standing in triumph. Why not shoot an arrow at him and make an end of him? Come, take my advice and do so. Fit the arrow to the string, and then pray to Apollo, the god of Archery."

Pandarus was foolish enough to allow himself to be persuaded. He took out his great bow from its case. It was made out of the horns of an ibex which he himself had shot in the mountains. The horns measured sixteen hands, and they had been fitted together by a clever craftsman, who had polished them and given them golden tips. Pandarus pressed down the bow and strung it. Then, while his companions held their shields in front of him, he chose out a keen arrow that had never yet been used and fitted it to the string. He made his prayer to Apollo, then, holding tightly the notched end of the arrow and the bow-string he drew them back till the string touched his breast and the iron head of the arrow was on the curve of the bow. Taking careful aim, he loosed the arrow. The bow twanged; the string sang like a swallow and the piercing arrow leapt eagerly through the air among the press of men.

But the blessed immortal Gods did not forget Menelaus. Athene herself stood by him and warded off the arrow, turning it aside from the vital parts, as a mother brushes a fly aside from her child's sleeping face. The sharp point struck upon the golden clasps of his belt and pierced right through them. It pierced the armour underneath, and the tunic beneath the armour. The wound was a slight one, but still the purple blood gushed out over Menelaus's thighs and legs, running down over his well-shaped ankles.

Agamemnon shuddered when he saw the black blood. "O my brother," he cried, "are our oaths and our promises to end in your death? The day will come, I am sure of it, when Priam's city of Troy will fall into our hands. But what good will that be, if before then you have lost your life? How could I bear to return to Argos without you, my brother?"

But Menelaus comforted him and said: "All is well, my brother. Say nothing to discourage the army. My belt and my armour have taken the full force of the arrow and the wound can be cured."

Then Agamemnon sent for the famous doctor Machaon, who examined the wound and washed it and put upon it some healing ointment which once the wise centaur Chiron had given to his father Asclepius.

Meanwhile the men on both sides were standing to their arms. The gods themselves were there to urge them into battle. On the Trojan side was Ares, god of War, breathing his spirit of dreadful violence into the army; and with the Greeks was the grey-eyed goddess Athene, no less resolute

in her own cause. Now there were no thoughts of peace.
Each side was full of hatred for the other, each longing to
hear the groaning of men in their death agony.

Agamemnon went along the ranks of the Greeks, urging
them on to battle. "Our enemies have broken the truce,"
he shouted, "and now Father Zeus will protect them no
longer. Instead their smooth flesh will be devoured by the
vultures and the dogs. We shall sack their city and take their
women and children for our slaves." So he spoke, little
knowing the trouble in store for his men, and for himself.

And now the two armies met together with a noise like
thunder in the mountains. Shield pressed on shield; spears
tore their way through armour; swords clashed together.
Of the men who fell in that first onset one was a son of Priam.
Great Odysseus struck him down with his long spear and
his armour rang out as he writhed on the ground in death.
And as Odysseus plunged forward the whole Trojan line
began to give way. But the god Apollo, the friend of the
Trojans, cried out to them: "Forward, horsemen and
charioteers of Troy. These Greeks are not made of stone or
iron. They have flesh that can feel your weapons. Moreover
Achilles, the son of Thetis, is not with them. He is nursing
his anger by his ships."

So Apollo put fresh heart into the Trojans, who surged
forward again into battle, while on the other side the goddess
Athene was encouraging the Greeks.

VI

THE DEEDS OF DIOMEDES

IT WAS on this day that Athene gave to Diomedes, the great son of Tydeus, such strength and valour and audacity that he stood out above all the other warriors and won for himself immortal fame. He raged through the Trojan ranks like a wild lion, and his shield and helmet shone like that star which in the summer months is brighter than all other stars as it rises washed from the streams of Ocean.

So Trojan after Trojan fell before the spear of Diomedes. He stripped the armour from their bodies and gave their horses to his followers, who drove them back to his ships. He himself pressed on with the attack and wherever he went the enemy fell back before him.

Now when Pandarus saw Diomedes come raging over the plain like a winter torrent that sweeps away the hedges and the dykes, driving whole companies of men before him, he bent his bow, fitted an arrow to the string and shot him in the right shoulder. The point pierced through the plates of his armour and the black blood spouted out over his breast. Pandarus shouted out in triumph: "See, Trojans, the best of the Greeks is wounded, nor will he last long, I think. Now, forward again into battle and drive them before you!"

But Diomedes was not for long out of the action. He withdrew a little from the battle and his faithful charioteer, Sthenelus, pulled the arrow out of his shoulder and bound up the wound from which the blood gushed out. Then

Diomedes prayed to Athene: "O daughter of Zeus, just as you used to help my father in his battles, now, I pray you, help me. Let me kill Pandarus. Let him come within reach of my spear. So far he has only shot at me from a distance and now he is boasting that I shall soon be dead."

Athene heard his prayer and came to stand at his side. "Diomedes," she said, "fear nothing. Now I have filled your heart with all the courage of your father, he who once fought single handed with fifty men and killed them all. And I have also taken the mist from your eyes so that you can tell the difference between men and gods. You may fight against any man, but, if the gods join in the battle, do not fight against them—or only against one of them. If Aphrodite comes to the war, you may wound her with your sharp spear."

Athene vanished from his sight and Diomedes once more charged into the front line. Now he was three times as fierce and bold as he had been before. He hacked men's arms from their shoulders; he dragged men backwards from their chariots; each throw of his spear stretched a champion on the bloody ground. He was like a wounded lion ravaging a sheep fold from which the shepherd has fled in terror.

The Trojan prince Aeneas saw him from the part of the field where he too was fighting bitterly. He went at once to find Pandarus and, when he had found him, said: "Pandarus, now is the time for you to use your bow and arrows. Are you not said to be the best archer in Lycia, better than all the archers of Troy? Now show what you can do and shoot down that man over there, whoever he is."

Pandarus answered him. "The man you mean is Diomedes. I recognise him by his shield and his helmet. But he seems to be protected by some god. I have shot at him already and hit him in the right shoulder. I thought that I had killed him. Never before have I had such bad luck with my bow. Now I wish that I had taken the advice of my father who, before I left home to come to Troy, was always telling me to leave my bow behind and to fight from a chariot. I have eleven fine chariots standing idle in my father's palace, and swift horses to go with them. I wish I had taken them instead of this unlucky bow with which today I have wounded two of the best of the Greeks. But now both Menelaus and Diomedes are back again in the battle. I have a good mind to break my bow in two and burn it."

"If it is a chariot and horses you want," said Aeneas, "let us use mine. They are the best horses in Troy and come from an immortal stock. You may drive them and let me meet Diomedes with my spear. Or, if you prefer, I will drive the horses and let you do the fighting."

"The horses know you," said Pandarus. "It would be better for you to drive them. I have failed with my bow. Let me see now what I can do with my spear."

So they mounted the chariot and drove fast towards Diomedes. Sthenelus, the charioteer, saw them coming and cried out: "Diomedes, my dear friend, be careful of your life. You have fought enough already. Here come two great champions against you. One is Pandarus and the other is Prince Aeneas."

Diomedes looked at him sternly: "Do not talk to me of fear," he said. "My strength is still with me. But, if I strike down these men, make sure that you seize their horses. They are the best horses in the world and come from a race of horses that Zeus himself gave to the first king of Troy. I mean to have them for myself."

As he spoke Aeneas and Pandarus were upon him. Pandarus hurled his heavy spear and the point tore through the shield of Diomedes, reaching the armour underneath. Then Pandarus shouted out: "I have struck him, right through the side. He cannot last long now, and now I shall have the glory that I prayed for."

But his boasting was in vain. Strong Diomedes stared at him grimly. "My body is untouched," he said. "I think

that you will not escape so easily from this spear of mine."
So saying, he poised his spear and threw it. It struck
Pandarus on the nose by the eye, and the point went through
his teeth, cutting off the tongue at the root, and came out
in his throat below the chin. Pandarus fell headlong from
the chariot and, as his shining armour rang upon the ground,
the horses reared and shied in terror. So Pandarus died and was
more unlucky with the spear than he had been with the bow.

Now with a great shout Aeneas sprang down from the
chariot and stood over the dead body of Pandarus, covering
it with his shield and his spear. He seemed like a strong
lion at bay, as he stood there ready to face all who approached
him. Diomedes then picked up a great rock, so big that it
would have taken two ordinary men, such as men are today,
even to lift it. But Diomedes lifted it easily and hurled it at
Aeneas, striking him on the hip bone, tearing the muscles and
breaking the bone itself. Great Aeneas felt his legs give way
beneath him; he supported himself on the ground with one
hand, and darkness came over his eyes. Indeed he certainly
would have been killed there before he could recover himself,
if his mother Aphrodite had not seen the danger of her son.
She sped down from Olympus to his side and threw her
arms round him to protect him.

Diomedes recognised the goddess but still pressed forward. He thrust at her with his spear and pierced through
the fragrant robe that had been made for her by the Graces.
He wounded her on the wrist and out of the wound flowed
some of the ichor, or immortal blood, that runs in the veins
of the gods. Aphrodite screamed with pain and dropped the
body of her son. She fled from the battle, and as she fled,
Diomedes shouted after her: "Daughter of Zeus, it would
be better to leave war alone in future. Is it not enough for
you to be spending your time in breaking the hearts of weak
defenceless women? Leave warfare to men."

As for Aphrodite, she fled back to Olympus to the palace
of Father Zeus and there she complained of the treatment

she had received. But Hera and Athene mocked at her and Athene said: "It looks as though Aphrodite has been persuading some other woman to desert her husband, and has somehow managed to scratch her slender hand on the woman's golden brooch."

Zeus smiled at this and said to Aphrodite: "My dear child, war is not your business. You should leave that to Athene or to Ares."

Meanwhile Diomedes was searching everywhere for Aeneas, but Apollo had taken him up from the ground and carried him to safety inside the city. Here he cured his wounds and soon the great warrior was back again in the fighting. But he had lost his famous horses, for Sthenelus had obeyed his master's orders and had driven them back to the tent of Diomedes.

And now the Trojans were being driven back towards their city walls. But powerful help was at hand for them. Apollo called to the war god himself, Ares, and said: "Ares, murderous god, you who sate yourself on the blood of men and rejoice in the noise of falling towers and of burning cities, come now and drive this man Diomedes from the battle and give your help to the Trojans."

Then Ares took upon himself the shape of one of the leaders of the Trojan allies. In the thick of the fighting he stood by Hector and urged him on against the Greeks. In his hand he held a tremendous spear and wherever he and Hector went Panic followed them. With this powerful aid Hector himself fought with twice his usual courage. Aeneas also was spurred on to even greater efforts, and now gradually the Greeks began to give way.

Diomedes recognised the War God fighting at Hector's side and he said to his followers: "My friends, we must retreat a little. See how Hector is destroying our men. But there is nothing strange in that, for Ares himself is with him. We cannot fight with the immortal gods. Fall back, therefore, but keep your faces to the enemy."

For some time the other Greek champions, Odysseus, Ajax, Menelaus and the rest stood like rocks against which the sea surges and beats, but finally they too had to give way before the Trojans. They retreated in good order, still fighting fiercely, but still, as they retreated, Hector killed man after man, and man after man fell before the great spear of Ares at his side.

From Olympus Hera and Athene saw how the Greeks were being driven back. They came in indignation to Father Zeus and said: "See how this murderous Ares is slaughtering the gallant Greeks. It is Apollo and Aphrodite who have let him loose. Will you not allow us to stop him and drive him from the battle?"

Zeus, since he hated the god of War and his savagery, gave his consent and the two goddesses came down to the plain and to the fighting. Hera put on the shape of Stentor, one of the Greeks who had a voice which was as loud as the voices of fifty men together. Using his voice she shouted out to the Greeks, urging them to resist and to fight back at the advancing Trojans. And Athene went to look for Diomedes. She found him a little withdrawn from the battle. He was cooling the wound which he had received from Pandarus, wiping away the blood, and had, for the time, laid aside his heavy shield, since, what with the sweat and the fighting, its straps were cutting into the flesh of his shoulders. Athene stood by him and said: "How different you are from your father Tydeus! He was smaller than you, but how he used to fight! Nothing would stop him. And now here you stand, in spite of the help I promised you, idle and useless! Are you tired already? Or are you afraid?"

"Goddess," said Diomedes, "I recognise you and will speak freely. I am neither tired nor frightened. I am only doing as you told me to do. You told me not to fight with any of the gods except with Golden Aphrodite. Now Ares is leading the Trojans and from him I ordered my men to fall back."

Athene smiled at him. "Dear Diomedes," she said, "I never doubted your courage. Now I am with you and you need not fear Ares or any other god. Be confident and drive straight at him in your chariot. He is a mad bully and a traitor. Only yesterday he promised Hera and me that he would fight on the Greek side, but now he has been won over by Aphrodite and Apollo."

With these words she took the place of Sthenelus in Diomedes' chariot. Sthenelus was glad enough to be relieved. She took the reins and the whip in her hands and drove the swift horses forward to the place where huge Ares, his face and arms spattered with the blood of the slain, was stripping the armour from a fallen Greek. Athene made herself invisible, but Ares saw Diomedes approach and came straight for him, brandishing his enormous spear. Over the horses' necks he thrust at Diomedes, but Athene caught the spear in her hand and pushed it upwards, so that it missed its mark. Then Diomedes thrust with his spear and Athene drove it forward to the lower part of the War God's belly. It struck home, and tore through the flesh. Diomedes drew the spear out of the wound, and, as he did so, Ares let out a great yell of agony, as loud as the noise made by nine or ten thousand men shouting together in battle. Both Greeks and Trojans stood still in terror as they heard the dreadful sound. And Diomedes saw for a moment the face of the War God twisted in agony. Then like a rushing black cloud of storm he swept upwards and away into the broad heaven.

In Olympus, still clutching his wound, he came before Father Zeus and began to complain. "Father Zeus," he said, "are you not shocked at the way your daughter Athene is behaving? Can you not control her? See how she rouses mortals against the gods. If I had not managed to escape, I might be lying there now on the plain among the dead bodies."

"Don't come whimpering to me," said Zeus, "you, who are always changing sides. You are the god whom I dislike most of all, since you enjoy nothing except violence and fighting. Also you are as bad-tempered and ungovernable as your mother Hera. But since you are my son I will cure your wound. Otherwise I should have done nothing for you at all."

So Zeus called for a divine ointment which healed immediately the wounded flesh of Ares, who bathed himself, put on fresh clothing, and sat down sulking among the gods.

Meanwhile Hera and Athene also withdrew from the fighting, and still the battle swayed backwards and forwards on the plain.

VII

HECTOR PREPARES FOR BATTLE

ALL DAY they fought, and at nightfall the Trojans withdrew within their city, while the Greeks went back to their ships. Heralds carried messages from one side to the other and it was agreed that there should be a truce while each army collected its own dead for burial. And so throughout the night, by the glow of innumerable fires, the dead bodies were brought back either to Troy or to the Greek camp. Men wept great tears as they dragged from the bloody plain the bodies of friends and companions in arms. In Troy itself there were wives, sisters, mothers and aged fathers to mourn over their dear ones, but the families of the Greeks were far away beyond the echoing sea and beyond the ranges of many mountains.

And now Zeus summoned the immortal gods and spoke to them. "Listen to me," he said, "and abide by what I say. I will not allow any of you any more to take part in the fighting. It is decreed by Fate that no help is to reach the Greeks until they are fighting among their own ships. This is also my will, and it must be obeyed. I warn you that if any one of you disobeys me, that one will be hurled out of heaven with the blast of my thunderbolts."

The gods listened in silence. Hera and Athene indeed would have wished to argue with the Almighty Father, but his look was so severe and his words had been so full of force that they did not dare to speak openly. Afterwards indeed they complained to each other. "This is the doing of

Thetis," they said, "who has won Zeus over to her side in order to avenge her son Achilles." But there was nothing that they could do against the clear orders of the Father of Gods and Men.

Early in the morning the warriors armed themselves and prepared for battle. After the fighting of the day before the Greeks felt certain that Priam's great city was almost in their hands. On the other side the Trojans and their allies were determined to resist.

In Troy Hector summoned the captains and the princes to battle. When fully armed himself he came to the palace of Paris, and found Paris himself with Helen sitting beside him in their gorgeous bedroom. Paris was still looking at his beautiful armour and was testing his curved bow in his hands. Hector looked at him sternly. "Still not ready for battle?" he said. "Yet all this fighting has come upon us because of you. Other men are dying for you at our very walls. Do you intend to wait here until the city itself is on fire?"

"Hector," said Paris, "what you say is quite right. Indeed I should have been ready before, and now Helen also has just been urging me to join in the battle. I agree with you both, and I think that today things will go better than they did yesterday. Will you not wait a moment for me to get ready? If you cannot, I will hurry and catch you up before you leave the town."

Hector made no reply to this, but Helen spoke softly to him and said: "Dear brother Hector, I am indeed a shameless wicked creature. I wish that a storm had carried me away on the very day that I was born and had hurled me into the middle of the sea. Then I should not have come here to cause such trouble to you and to my own people as well. And my next wish would be to have had a better husband than this man. For he pays no attention at all to the reproaches of others. But now come in and sit down for a moment. It is you who have to bear all the worry and the toil of battle for the sake of faithless me and my accursed husband."

"Helen," said Hector, "I thank you for your kindness. But you must not ask me to come and sit down now. My place is with the army who miss me if I am not there. Make your husband hurry, so that he can catch me up before I leave the city. Now I am going to my own home to say good-bye to my wife Andromache and to my little boy Astyanax."

So Hector went to his home, but he did not find his wife there. She had been to the temple to pray for her husband's safety, and now she was waiting by the Scaean Gate to speak to him before he led out the Trojans to the plain. She saw him coming from a distance and she hurried towards him. Behind her came a maid carrying the little boy in her arms. Hector smiled as he saw his son, but he said nothing. Andromache put her hand in his. As she spoke the tears flooded to her eyes. "Dear husband," she said, "must you always be fighting? Will you not think of your child and your wife? We could not live without you. And now, if you stand every day in the front of battle, there will surely be a time when all the Greeks will attack you at once and kill you. I would rather die than be without you. Indeed I have no one else left. My father was king in woody Thebe, but Achilles took his city and killed him, though he was too noble a man to strip him of his arms, and he gave him an honourable burial. Afterwards the nymphs planted elm trees around his tomb. I had seven brothers too, and all of these were killed by great Achilles in one day. At the same time he took my mother prisoner, and, though he allowed us to ransom her, she died afterwards in our house. So you, Hector, are father and mother and brothers to me, as well as my dear husband. Have pity on us. Do not leave your wife a widow and your child an orphan. Stay here today on the tower and defend the city from here."

"If I were to behave like a coward," said Hector, "I should be ashamed to meet the Trojans and their wives and daughters. In any case I could not do as you say. I have learnt not to give in, but always to stand in the front ranks, winning fame for my father and for myself. Nevertheless somehow deep down in my heart I know that the day will come when holy Troy and Priam and his people will be destroyed. And I do not feel so much pain for the fate of Priam or of Hecuba or of all my brave brothers who will be beaten down into the dust as I feel for your sake, and at the thought of some Greek dragging you off to slavery. I cannot bear to think of you in Greece, working in another man's house, with people pointing at you and saying: 'That is the wife of Hector, who led the Trojans in the fighting around Troy.' And your sorrow will come over you again as you feel the lack of me who would have protected you. I pray that I may lie deep in my grave at that time, and not hear your cries as you are dragged away."

As he finished speaking Hector turned to his little boy to take him in his arms. But the child cried and buried his head in his nurse's breast. He was frightened at the sight of his father in his glittering armour with the great helmet and the horsehair crest nodding dreadfully above it. Both Hector and Andromache laughed, and famous Hector took the helmet from his head and put it down upon the ground. Then he kissed his son and swung him to and fro in his arms. He prayed also to Zeus and to the other immortal gods. "Zeus and all you gods," he said, "I pray you make this boy like me, strong and brave, a famous King of Troy. And when he comes back from battle let people say of him: 'Here comes one who is an even better soldier than his father was'."

Then Hector kissed his wife and said to her: "Dear wife, you must not alarm yourself about me. No one will send me to Hades before my time. But no man alive, however brave or however cowardly, can escape what fate has in store for him. And now you must go back to the house and see to your work there. War is men's business."

So Hector took up his helmet and his spear. Andromache went back to her house and, as she went, she often turned round to look at him and great tears fell from her eyes. When she got home, she and her servants all mourned for him, for they thought that he would never come back alive from the battle.

Meanwhile Paris had caught Hector up. Now he too was fully armed, but he excused himself for being late. "Brother," said Hector to him, "you can fight well enough. Only you are apt to give in too soon and not keep on to the end. Now let us go. Fight well today, and I shall hold nothing against you if Zeus and the immortal gods allow us to return in victory."

So Hector led the army out into the plain and in front of them was the army of the Greeks drawn up for battle. Now Zeus thundered from Olympus and the warriors stood still, not knowing what the omen might mean or to which side Zeus would give his aid.

VIII

A TROJAN VICTORY

AND NOW once again the two great forces hurtled together and the air was filled with the noise of clashing shields and swords, of the whinnying of horses and of the cries of the wounded and of the dying. All through the morning of this day men fell on either side in the rain of spears and arrows and in fighting hand-to-hand. But in the afternoon Zeus gave fresh strength to the Trojans and the line of the Greeks began to waver. No more could great Agamemnon, or Ajax or Idomeneus hold their ground, as Hector led his men in charge after charge against them. They began to retreat over the plain backwards in the direction of the wall and deep ditch that protected their ships.

But old Nestor was left behind in the retreat. One of his chariot horses had been shot in the head by Paris and now this horse, plunging and writhing on the ground, had made it impossible to control the other two horses that drew the shining chariot. Nestor himself had drawn his sword and was hacking at the reins in order to free the wounded animal, when he saw Hector himself in all the pride of his victory come driving towards him over the plain.

Then certainly the old King Nestor would have lost his life and Hector would have taken from him the famous shield that he carried, if Diomedes had not seen his peril. Quickly he drove up to Nestor and said to him, "My old friend, you are not a match for these young warriors. Your horses are too slow. Come and take the reins in my chariot. You will see how swift are these Trojan horses that I took yesterday from Aeneas. Let our charioteers look after your horses while you and I stand against Hector, and let us show him that my spear is as thirsty for blood as is his own."

Old Nestor was willing enough. He took the reins and drove the horses towards Hector who himself was yearning for the fight. Diomedes was the first to throw his spear. He missed Hector but struck his charioteer right through the breast so that he fell out of the chariot and threw the horses into a panic. And now Diomedes would have pressed on, but from Mount Ida there came a sudden roar of thunder and Zeus hurled down a thunderbolt which tore into the earth in front of the horses that Nestor was driving. The air was full of the smell of sulphur. The horses shied and reared up in terror. Nestor, terrified himself, turned to Diomedes and said: "Diomedes, it is no use fighting against Zeus. We must turn the horses round and fly. There is no help for it. Zeus is more powerful than we are."

"You are right," said Diomedes, "but I cannot bear the thought that soon Hector will be boasting over us and saying: 'Diomedes could not face me in battle. He was so frightened that he ran to his ships.' "

"Both Trojans and Greeks," said Nestor, "know well that you are no more a coward than was your father Tydeus. But today Zeus is allowing Hector to do what he wishes with us."

Then Nestor turned the horses and they drove back in flight after the rest of the Greeks towards the ditch and fortifications that guarded their camp. As they went the Trojans shouted in triumph and surged after them. Hector cried out to his men: "See how Diomedes, the best warrior of them all, is running away like a woman. Now is the time to make certain of our victory. Their wretched walls will be no defence to them, and as for their ditch our horses can easily jump it. Let me but once get among their hollow ships. I shall burn the ships with fire and cut down the men as they go staggering about in the smoke."

Then Hector called to his chariot horses and spoke to them by name. "Xanthus," he said, "and you, Podargus, and Aithon, and noble Lampus, now is the time to repay me for all the care and kindness which you have received from Andromache; for she always gave you your food of honeyed wheat and mixed wine and water for you to drink, and saw that you were satisfied before she gave me my food, although I am her husband. Now put out all your speed. Let us see whether we can capture Nestor's famous shield and the great breastplate of Diomedes which was made for him by the god Hephaestus."

So speaking, he swept upon the fleeing Greeks. Nestor and Diomedes indeed escaped, helped as they were by the swift horses of Aeneas, but in the space between the ships and the surrounding trench chariots and men were huddled together in a disorderly mass, and among them the sword and spear of Hector fell like lightning, as he raged forward irresistibly, determined to set fire among the ships. And indeed he might have done so that very day if Hera had not put it into the heart of Agamemnon to rally the troops once more.

Agamemnon stood by the black ship of Odysseus, which was in the middle of the line of ships, and he shouted out so that his voice carried far along the whole line. "Shame upon you, Greeks!" he shouted, "What has happened to us? What has happened to all our boasting? We used to say that each one of us was a match for a hundred Trojans, and now the whole lot of us cannot stand up to this one Hector. O Father Zeus, has there ever been another great king who was so cast down from his hopes and from his glory? At least grant me this prayer. Save my army from utter destruction."

Zeus heard the prayer of Agamemnon. He put fresh heart into the Greeks. Diomedes sallied out again beyond the wall, and with him were Agamemnon and Menelaus, Ajax and his brother Teucer. Teucer stood under the cover of his brother's shield, and, looking out from under this protection, he would shoot his arrows among the Trojans, each time picking out one of their foremost champions. Eight of them he shot down, one after the other. Then he aimed an arrow at Hector. This time he missed his mark but he hit one of the sons of Priam, who dropped dead in the dust, with his head falling over sideways like the head of a poppy in a garden when it is weighed down by its seed and by the moisture of a summer shower. "Let me try again," said Teucer, "to kill this mad dog," and once more he aimed an arrow at Hector. But Apollo turned the point aside, and the arrow struck Hector's charioteer full in the breast, so that he fell headlong from the chariot.

In grief and fury for his loss, Hector leapt to the ground. Teucer was just fitting another arrow to his bow, but Hector picked up a great jagged piece of rock and hurled it at him before he had time to take aim. He struck him on the collar bone, numbing his whole arm and shoulder. The bow dropped from his hands and he sank down on his knees. His life was saved however, since great Ajax covered him with his shield while his comrades lifted him up and carried him back to the ships.

And now once more the Trojans drove forward and the Greeks were pressed back to the trench that they desperately attempted to defend. That day they were saved by the coming of night, for now the bright sun set in the stream of Ocean and drew darkness over the earth. Hector, though unwillingly, was forced to withdraw his troops, while the weary Greeks thanked the immortal gods for this respite from the bitter fighting.

Hector did not lead his army back to the city. Instead he called an assembly in the plain near the river, where the ground was not covered with dead bodies. "Listen to me," he said, "my Trojans and my gallant allies! I thought that this day we would set fire to the Greek ships and destroy these invaders. They have been saved by darkness and not by any courage of their own. Now we shall camp here in the plain and at daybreak tomorrow we shall attack and not cease till we have driven them into the sea. Meanwhile let men go back to Troy and bring us out sheep and oxen for our evening meal. Let them bring wood too, so that we may have fires to burn all night long. Guards must be set, and we must keep an eye on the enemy, in case they may try to escape this very night. Tomorrow we will attack in full force, and I wish I were as certain that I should never die or grow old as I am certain that tomorrow will be a day of evil for the Greeks."

The Trojans shouted their applause and did as Hector commanded. They unharnessed their sweating horses and tethered them by their chariots. Wood and provisions were brought from the city. Soon their innumerable watch fires sparkled over the plain, like the stars shining around the moon on a windless night when all the mountain tops and headlands and rocky defiles stand out clearly and the great spaces of the upper air yawn open in their fathomless extent, so that every star in heaven is shining and the shepherd rejoices. So shone the Trojan fires between the ships and the stream of Scamander. A thousand fires were burning, and round each of them sat fifty men in the gleaming fire-light. The horses stood by their chariots, munching the white barley. So they waited for the dawn.

IX

THE EMBASSY TO ACHILLES

ND NOW, while Hector and the Trojans planned the assault which on the next morning they would make upon the Greek camp, the Greeks themselves and all their leaders suffered a grief and a despair which were almost unendurable. Not only had they failed to take Troy upon that day, but they had lost numbers of their best men and now they were penned within the fortifications of their own camp.

When the sentries had been posted on the walls Agamemnon called a Council of the chief men in his army. As he rose to speak the tears poured from his eyes. "Zeus," he said, "has been the most cruel of the gods to me. He promised that we would bring down the high walls of Troy, but now he has changed his mind and is giving the victory to Hector. What are we to do? Are we to get on board our ships tonight and sail back to Argos, or are we to remain here till the ships are burnt and we ourselves are slaughtered by our ships?"

The others listened to the king in silence. Then Diomedes rose to speak. "Agamemnon," he said, "you are free to run away if you like, and so are all the rest of the long-haired Greeks. But I shall never give in, no, not if you all go back to Argos. I and Sthenelus, my charioteer, shall still stay here and fight, even if we have to fight alone."

This speech of Diomedes put fresh heart into the Greeks, and they shouted out that they too would stay and fight to the end. Then old Nestor spoke. "My lord Agamemnon," he said, "I am an old man, and it is right for you, great king as you are, to listen to my advice. The noble Diomedes has spoken well. He is a true son of his father Tydeus, whom I remember well in my young days. But here is another thing that we can do. It was because of your action, King Agamemnon, that we have been without the help of great Achilles, whom Zeus loves so much that he will not protect us now that Achilles is out of the fighting. Will you not now be reconciled with him and offer him gifts if he will relent from his anger? I think that today's battle would have gone very differently if Achilles had been on our side."

To this Agamemnon replied: "Nestor, what you have said is true. It was the gods who drove me to that state of mad folly when I quarrelled with Achilles. And now I will tell you what I will do to satisfy him and to make up for my insults to him. I will give him back the girl Briseis whom I took from him and with her I will send seven women of great beauty and skilled in all kinds of useful work, women whom I took prisoners on the island of Lesbos. I will give him also ten talents of gold, twenty shining cauldrons, and twelve fine racehorses all of which have won prizes. All this I will give him now, and later on, if the gods allow us to sack the great city of Priam, let him fill his ship with gold and take the pick of the spoil. And when we return to Greece I will offer him my daughter in marriage and will honour him no less than I honour Orestes, my son. And with my daughter I will give him riches and seven of my finest towns, all lying near the sea coast. Let him only relent and put an end to the quarrel and serve with me again. He ought to do so. No man has a right to be always unyielding."

"Lord Agamemnon," said Nestor, "you have spoken well and generously. Now let us send to Achilles some of our best men to tell him of your offer. We have with us old Phoenix whom Peleus, Achilles' father, made tutor and guardian to his son. He must go now and use his influence.

Great Ajax should go also and wise Odysseus with his soothing words."

To this proposal all the others agreed. Phoenix went at once to Achilles, but Ajax and Odysseus first had their supper and then walked together to the camp of the Myrmidons along the shore of the breaking sea. As they went they prayed to Poseidon, the god of the sea, that their words might be able to soften the proud heart of Achilles.

Soon they came to his tent and there they found Achilles playing on a lyre and delighting himself with the songs he sang of the great deeds of heroes. Opposite him sat Patroclus with his eyes fixed on his friend's face as he waited for him to finish the song. Phoenix too was in the tent, but he had not yet spoken with his old pupil.

Odysseus, with Ajax following him, stepped forward and Achilles immediately sprang to his feet, still holding the lyre in his hand, and hurried to greet them. "Welcome," he said, "to you both. Of all the Greeks you are the two whom I love most, and I am happy to have you under my roof. And now, Patroclus, you must bring out bigger cups and better wine. For these two are some of my greatest friends."

Patroclus did as his friend asked him. They all sat down together in the firelight and poured out their libations to the immortal gods. Then Ajax nodded his head to Phoenix, encouraging him to speak, but Odysseus in fact spoke first and said: "Achilles, I drink to you and wish you well and thank you for your hospitality. And yet we are in no mood for eating and drinking. Today we have only just escaped with our lives and tomorrow we may lose them. Hector and his arrogant Trojans have carried everything before them and have beaten us back to our ships. And now they wait eagerly for the dawn and Hector is already boasting that tomorrow he will burn our ships with fire and butcher us beside them. Will you not rouse yourself, therefore, and help us in our need? Will you not forget your quarrel with

THE EMBASSY TO ACHILLES

Agamemnon, who now is ready to offer you every honour and a hundred times the value of what he took from you?"

Here Odysseus paused and then, speaking slowly, he told Achilles of what Agamemnon had promised to give him. Finally he said: "And if, Achilles, you are not moved by the gifts of King Agamemnon, then think of us other Greeks in the army. Think of how we should honour you if you came now to help us. Think too that now is the time when you might win immortal fame by killing great Hector himself in all his confidence. For now he would fight with the gods themselves."

But here Achilles interrupted him. "Odysseus," he said, "my noble and wise friend, let me tell you at once how my mind stands. For I hate like hell itself the man who keeps his intentions secret and says something different from what he means. Not Agamemnon nor all the rest of the Greeks will ever make me change my mind. I have stayed awake all night and I have fought all day in his service, and what reward did I get for it? He has injured me and I shall never forgive him. If now he wants to save his life, he must depend on you and the others. As for me, I shall sail back to my own country and be happy there. Tell him that I do not want his gifts, that I do not want to marry his daughter. All over Greece there are beautiful and noble women whom I might marry and with whom I could live happily and at peace. Now I think that life itself is worth more than all the wealth that Troy enjoyed in the days of peace before the Greeks came here—more than all the gold in Apollo's temple at Delphi, or the fabulous riches of Egyptian Thebes. The goddess, my mother, has told me that Fate has given me the choice of two roads—either to fight here and never to return home, or else to live quietly in my own land and be happy, though not famous for ever. Now I shall go home and I advise you also to do so. This is my last word, and I should wish you to report it to the Greeks tonight. But Phoenix can stay here with me, and, if he wishes, take ship with me in the morning."

When Achilles ceased speaking the others remained for some time in silence, looking anxiously at each other; for Achilles had refused them utterly. Finally the old warrior Phoenix spoke. The tears fell from his eyes, so much he feared for the Greek ships. "Dear child," he said, "will you not listen to me? Will you not remember how your father Peleus put you into my care? I have always loved you as though you were my own son, and you loved me too. When you were a little boy you would never take your food from any hand but mine. You have often sat on my knee and spilt wine over my clothes when you were learning how to eat and drink. And later, when we came to this lamentable war, your father begged you to be guided by me, since he knew that I would never give you bad advice. Even now, if Agamemnon had not shown that he was ready to yield to you, I should not be advising you to accept his offers. But Agamemnon repents. He offers you great gifts and he has sent to you the noblest men among the Greeks, who are your friends, in order to show his respect. My child, it is not right to be so unyielding. Even the gods yield to prayers, and prayers indeed are the daughters of Zeus who go about the world seeking to do good. It is right to receive them into our hearts. Think too of how the Greeks will honour you, if you save them in their great peril. I beg you, dear child, to be persuaded."

But Achilles replied to him, "Old friend, my mind is made up. It is no use trying to touch my heart by recalling old times and so taking the part of Agamemnon whom I hate. Nor do I care what the Greeks think of me. I have sworn not to join in the fighting though all the ships go up in fire, unless Hector is so bold as to attack my own men and my own ships. Now I advise you to stay the night here, and tomorrow we will decide whether to sail home or not."

Ajax then turned to Odysseus and said: "Great Odysseus, let us be going. We must tell the others our news, bad as it is, since they are waiting for us. As for Achilles, his heart is as hard as a rock, and he will not listen to us, though we honour him and wish to show ourselves his friends."

So Ajax and Odysseus left Achilles in his tent and Phoenix with him. They went back on the way that they had come and found King Agamemnon and the other leaders of the Greeks eagerly awaiting them. When Odysseus told them of how the spirit of Achilles was still utterly unyielding and how he refused to join in the battle, there was a long silence. Finally Diomedes spoke and said: "Agamemnon, your generous offers have only made Achilles prouder than he was before. Let him go, I say. And tomorrow all of us must fight in the front line, encouraging our men by our example. There are others beside Achilles who are not afraid of Hector, and there are gods also on our side."

X

A RAID ON THE TROJAN CAMP

THEN THE rest of the leaders of the Greeks went to their ships, and, having seen that the sentries were posted, refreshed themselves with sleep. But Agamemnon could not sleep, so many were the thoughts that came to his mind and tormented it. Sometimes he looked out over the plain and saw the fires of the Trojan army encamped outside their city. There were countless fires burning, and from the Trojan camp came the noise of flute playing and of singing. And then when Agamemnon turned his eyes towards his own army and towards the Greek ships, he tore his hair and he wept bitterly at the thought of the danger that surrounded them. Finally, in his sleepless mood, he left his bed, bound his bright sandals on his feet, threw over his shoulders a great lion skin cloak that reached to his ankles, and, taking his spear in his hand, set out in the night in order to consult old Nestor and to discuss with him the plans for the morrow's battle.

But he had not gone far from his tent when he was met by his brother Menelaus. Menelaus too had found it impossible to sleep, and now the brothers decided to call yet another council of war in the tent of Nestor. Agamemnon went one way and Menelaus another. They woke all the great captains of the army and all met together quietly, while the troops were still sleeping, near the place where Nestor's black ships were drawn up on the shore.

Now when they were all together Nestor spoke. "Is there any of us," he said, "who has the courage to go out towards the Trojan camp and find out what their plans are? It would greatly help us to know whether they intend to stay where they are or to return to the city before attacking us in the morning. A brave man, willing to take the risk, might steal into their camp, and perhaps take a prisoner who could give us news. Such a man would not only be honoured by us, but would also be properly rewarded."

He paused and immediately Diomedes replied to him. "Nestor," he said, "I am willing to take on this adventure. But I should like it better if someone would come with me. In these affairs two are better than one."

Many of the Greeks immediately volunteered to go with Diomedes into the Trojan camp. There were Menelaus, Ajax, Odysseus and many others. Out of these Agamemnon told Diomedes to choose as comrade the one whom he would prefer himself. In his heart he hoped that he would not choose his brother Menelaus, since the task was dangerous. Diomedes did not hesitate. "Since you allow me," he said, "to choose my own comrade, I shall choose the godlike Odysseus. He is ready to take any risk and he keeps a stout heart in all difficulties. Moreover Pallas Athene loves him. He and I could go through fire together and come out safe. He is full of resource and has a brain like lightning."

"There is no need," said Odysseus, "to talk about me. These men here know both my virtues and my faults. Let us be going. Most of the night has gone and we have no time to waste."

Then Diomedes borrowed from one of the others a great two-edged sword, since he had left his own sword in his tent. On his head he put a leather helmet, without plume or crest. Odysseus borrowed from the hero Meriones a sword, a bow and a cunningly made helmet. Inside it were a number of leather straps, so that it fitted tightly to the head, and the outside was decorated with rows of white boars' tusks.

So the two men went out and as they went Pallas Athene sent them a lucky omen, a heron on the right. They could not see the heron in the darkness, but they heard it croak. Then Odysseus prayed to Athene and said: "Hear me, daughter of Zeus, you who always stand at my side in danger, you whose notice I can never escape. Help me tonight and bring us back safe to the ships after we have done some great deed and made the Trojans suffer."

Diomedes also prayed to the goddess. "Hear me too," he said, "daughter of Zeus, and stand by me as once you stood by my father Tydeus when the Thebans set an ambush for him and he killed fifty of them with his own hand, because you supported him. Support me now, and when I return I will sacrifice to you a broad-browed heifer with horns gilded for the sacrifice."

So they prayed and Athene heard their prayers, for of all men these two were the ones whom she loved most. Then they went on like two lions in the black night, treading among the dead bodies, the blood and the abandoned weapons on the ground.

Meanwhile in the Trojan camp Hector also had been making his plans. He had called together a meeting of the Trojans and had offered great rewards to anyone who would go as a spy among the Greek ships, to find out whether the ships were guarded or whether the Greeks, after their defeat, were thinking of sailing away.

Among the Trojans there was a man called Dolon, a rich man, not handsome to look at, but fast on his feet. It was he who undertook the adventure. "I shall go right through the Greek camp," he said, "to the tent of Agamemnon, and I shall bring you back the news you want. Only I ask for my reward the horses and chariot of Achilles, since these are the best there are in the Greek army."

Hector, in his confidence, replied: "No other Trojan except you shall ride behind those horses. I swear it by Zeus himself."

Then Dolon slung his curved bow over his shoulders and put on his head a cap made of ferret-skin. He covered himself with a grey wolf skin as a cloak, took a spear in his hand and set out towards the Greek camp.

He went fast and Odysseus was aware of him in the distance. He whispered to Diomedes. "Here comes someone from the Trojan army either to spy on us or to rob some of the dead bodies on the plain. Let us allow him to go a little way past us. Then we will spring out on him and, if he runs, we will head him off from his own army and drive him towards our ships."

So they lay down and hid themselves among the dead bodies. Dolon never saw them, but ran past, and, when he had gone a little way they sprang to their feet and ran after him. He heard their footsteps and for a moment he stopped still, looking backwards, thinking that Hector had sent messengers after him with more instructions. Soon, however, he knew that they were enemies and turned to run. But Odysseus and Diomedes followed in his tracks like sharp-toothed hounds that chase a hare turning and twisting and screaming before them through the woods. And if Dolon tried to run towards the Trojan camp, they headed him off and drove him towards the Greek outposts. Finally Diomedes was within spear's throw and he cried out: "Stop, or else you will feel my spear in your back." At the same time he threw his spear, but deliberately missed the man. The bright weapon flew over his shoulder and stuck quivering in the ground. Now Dolon's courage failed him and he stopped still, shaking and shivering with fear, while Diomedes and Odysseus came up to him and tightly seized his arms. Dolon burst into tears and, as he spoke, his teeth chattered together. "Take me alive," he begged, "and I will promise you a great ransom. In my house I have stores of gold and bronze and well-shaped iron. Only spare my life."

Odysseus looked at him grimly and said: "We will speak of that later. Now answer my questions. What are you doing here? Was it Hector who sent you out to spy upon our camp?"

"Yes," said Dolon, "and he promised me the chariot and horses of Achilles if I came back with the news he wanted."

Odysseus smiled. "A great prize indeed," he said. "But those horses are difficult to manage and difficult to drive for anyone except Achilles himself. Now tell me in what part of the field did you leave Hector. In what way are the sentries posted? What are the plans for tomorrow?" Dolon, still terrified, answered the questions of Odysseus. Among other things he told him that the Trojan allies were sleeping separately from the main Trojan army and he pointed out the place where was the camp of the Thracians under their king, Rhesus. "Rhesus," said Dolon, "has the most beautiful and the biggest horses that I have ever seen. They are whiter than snow and run faster than the wind. His chariot too is made of silver and gold, and he has some wonderful golden armour, more suitable for gods than for men to wear. I promise you that I am telling the truth. You can leave me here bound and go and see for yourselves. I stake my life on it."

"There is no need for you to stake your life," said Diomedes, "since we shall take that in any case. If we spared you, you might come out to spy on our camp again."

Dolon was stretching out his hands and beginning to speak, but Diomedes struck him on the neck so great a blow with his sword that he cut off his head which fell in the dust with his lips still moving in speech.

They took his ferret skin cap, his bow and his cloak of wolf skin and Odysseus raised up these spoils to Athene and prayed to her. "Goddess," he said, "receive these spoils, since it was to you that first we prayed. And now help us as we go to raid the Thracian camp."

Then he hid the trophies under a tamarisk bush and he twisted reeds and marsh plants together at the top of the bush so as to mark it and make the place easy to recognise when they were on their way back.

And now they went forward again among the dead bodies and soon came to the place where the Thracians were encamped. There was no guard set and the men were sleeping quietly, overcome with the fatigue of fighting. Their armour was piled on the ground at their side, and by each man was a pair of horses. Rhesus himself was sleeping in the middle and his great white horses were tethered to the rail of his splendid chariot.

Odysseus whispered to Diomedes. "There is the man, and there are the horses that Dolon told us of. Now quickly draw your sword and start killing the men, or else leave that to me and get the horses out."

Diomedes sprang forward with his sword drawn and, like a lion falling upon a flock of sheep or goats, began a grim slaughter of men. On all sides was the noise of hideous groans and all the ground was red with blood. Twelve men Diomedes slew and, as he slew them, Odysseus took each body by the foot and dragged it aside so as to leave a way clear for the horses, since he feared that they might cause trouble by refusing to tread over the dead bodies of those who had tended them. King Rhesus himself was the thirteenth man whom Diomedes slew. He was breathing heavily in his sleep, since Athene had sent him a terrible dream. He dreamed that Diomedes, the son of Tydeus, was standing at his head, nor did he wake from the dream until his sweet life had left him.

Meanwhile Odysseus had tied the horses together with thongs and, using his bow as a whip, had driven them out into the open. Then he whistled to Diomedes, who came out to join him. They took a horse each, mounted, and rode back like the wind on the way by which they had come.

Scarcely had they gone when one of the Thracian leaders, a relation of King Rhesus, woke from sleep and saw the e mpty place where the horses had been. Then he saw the slaughter that Diomedes had made and the dead body of the king. He cried out and roused the whole camp. Hector with his Trojans came running up and they looked with amazement at the deeds which those two men had done.

Meanwhile the two rode on through the night, leaving the crying and the shouting behind them. When they reached the place where they had killed Dolon, Diomedes dismounted, took up the bloodstained arms which they had hidden, and gave them to Odysseus, so that later he might make an offering of them to Athene.

So they drew nearer to the Greek ships where the other leaders of the Greeks were anxiously awaiting them. It was old Nestor who first heard the sound of their approach. "My friends," he said to the others, "unless I am deceived, I hear the sound of horses. How good it would be if it were Odysseus and Diomedes riding in with horses captured from the enemy? Yet I fear it may be the Trojans themselves, and that something has happened to our best two warriors."

The words were hardly out of his mouth when the men themselves arrived. They jumped down from their horses laughing and their friends crowded round them and shook them by the hand. Nestor was the first to speak. "Glorious Odysseus," he said, "where did you get those horses? Never in my life have I seen finer ones. They shine like the sun. Did you really take them from the Trojans, or has some god given them to you? For Zeus loves you both, and so does Pallas Athene."

Odysseus answered him. "Nestor," he said, "the gods are stronger than we are, and a god, if he wanted, could give us even better horses than these. These we took from Rhesus, the King of Thrace. We killed him and twelve of his men; also on the way we killed a spy who was coming to our camp."

So, laughing, he drove the horses in among the Greek ships, and the other Greeks went with him, cheered by his success. Then they went into the sea to wash the sweat from their necks and thighs, and, after they had rubbed themselves down with olive oil, they took a meal and poured out to Athene libations of the cheerful wine.

XI

THE BATTLE IN THE PLAIN

BUT AS soon as Dawn had risen from her bed to bring light to gods and to men, the Greeks roused themselves for battle, knowing that now there must be no cowardice or hanging back from the fight if they were to keep Hector from setting fire to their ships upon that very day.

Agamemnon himself gave the call to arms. Then he put on his own armour of shining bronze. First he bound on his legs his beautiful greaves, fitted with silver over the ankles. Then he put on his breast the breastplate that had been sent him as a gift by the King of Cyprus when he heard of the sailing of the expedition to Troy. The breastplate was made of bands neatly fitted together—ten bands of dark blue enamel, twelve of gold and twenty of tin. At each side, reaching up to the place where the neck went through, were three coiling snakes, glittering with all the colours of the rainbow. Over his shoulders he slung his great sword, studded with gold on the hilt, and with a sheath of silver. Then he took up his huge man-covering shield. It was made of ten circles of bronze; the boss was of blue enamel and round this were twenty white shining studs of tin. On the shield was painted a Gorgon's head with grim eyes, and on each side were Terror and Panic. On his head Agamemnon put his helmet with its high crest and the horse hair plume dreadfully nodding above. In his hands he took up two strong well-pointed spears. So the King of Golden Mycenae went out shining into battle, and stood at the head of his army by the trench, with the chariots and the charioteers drawn up behind them, ready for action if they should push the Trojans back.

The Trojans on their side were marshalled by great Hector, by Aeneas, whom they honoured as a god, and by the three famous sons of Antenor. As he moved among his men, now here, now there, Hector in his blazing armour shone out fitfully like the lightning of Zeus, or like a baleful star that appears and reappears from behind the clouds.

And now the two armies fell upon each other like reapers in a rich man's field, cutting down the corn or barley in swathes. So all the morning men fell on each side and neither side would give way. But when it came to the time when a woodman in the hills would be weary of his task of felling trees and would begin to think of rest, then the Greeks began to break through the Trojan ranks and to force them back from the trench. Shouting to each other they pushed forward, and in front of them went Agamemnon, like a raging fire through the dry woods. Many were the captains and warriors whom he slew that day, and among them were two sons of Priam who had come out to battle in one chariot.

So the Trojans fell back before Agamemnon. By mid-day they had been pushed back to the old tomb of Ilus and the fig-tree half-way across the plain, and still Agamemnon pursued them, shouting his terrible war cry, his hands and unconquerable arms covered with the blood of those whom he had slain. On he swept, like a lion running amok among a herd of cattle at dusk, and he drove them back to the oak tree and the Scaean gate.

Zeus meanwhile was watching the battle. He had withdrawn Hector from the fighting and he sent to him his messenger Iris who came to him and said: "Hector, this is my message from Father Zeus. So long as you see Agamemnon in the front line, take no part in the fighting yourself, but order your men to hold firm and encourage them to do so. But once Agamemnon is wounded, Zeus will give strength to you and to the Trojans, so that you may kill and kill until you reach the Greek ships and until the darkness comes."

Hector then jumped down from his chariot and, taking two spears in his hand, went among the Trojan ranks, calling on them to stand firm and to yield no further ground. The Trojans obeyed him, and now in the forefront of their ranks, ready to meet the savage onset of Agamemnon, stood the two noble sons of Antenor, Iphidamas and Coön. Iphidamas had been brought up in distant Thrace, and the king who had brought him up there had offered him the hand of his daughter, so as to keep him always at home, so much he loved the youth for his beauty and his valour. But no sooner was the wedding over than Iphidamas heard of the expedition against Troy. He left his bride behind and came at once to fight against the Greeks.

Now he faced King Agamemnon and, thrusting at him with his spear, struck him full on the belt beneath the breast plate. But, though with all his weight he pressed his blow home, the spear point bent on the silver buckles of the belt. Agamemnon dragged the spear shaft out of his grasp and leapt towards him with his sword raised. He struck him on the neck so that his limbs were loosened and he fell to the ground in the sleep from which there is no waking. Hard indeed was his fate, dying there in defence of his country, far from the wife whom he had just married, but whose love he had never enjoyed.

And now Agamemnon began to strip the dead body of its glorious armour, but when Coön, the elder son of Antenor, saw what had happened to his brother, his eyes were dimmed with grief for it. He fell upon Agamemnon with his spear and struck him in the arm below the elbow. The point went clean through the flesh and Agamemnon shuddered as he felt the blow. Yet, wounded as he was, he did not give in. Coön had now taken hold of his brother's foot and was trying to drag the body back behind the Trojan lines. Agamemnon rushed at him and struck him with his spear below the shield. Then, springing forward, he cut off his head, there, upon the body of Iphidamas. So these two sons of Antenor both perished at the hands of Agamemnon.

And still, so long as the blood ran warm from his wound, Agamemnon pressed forward against the Trojans; but when the blood had dried and ceased to flow, the pain became unbearable and he could fight no longer. He mounted his chariot and ordered his charioteer to drive him back to the ships. As he went he cried out to the others: "Now it is for you, my friends, to fight on and save our ships. Zeus has not allowed me to fight all day."

Now when Hector saw that Agamemnon was wounded and was retiring from the battle, he shouted out with a great voice to the Trojans and their allies. "Now is the time to show our full strength. Now Zeus himself will give us the victory he had promised." And he plunged into the battle like a whirlwind that comes from the upper air and churns up the violet waters of the sea. Man after man he killed and behind him came the other Trojans, fired by his example.

The Greeks fell back and soon their retreat would have turned into a rout and they would have been driven again to their ships in that first onset if Odysseus had not called out across the ranks to Diomedes. "What has happened to us," he shouted, "in heaven's name? At this rate Hector will be among our ships before we know where we are. Come, my dear friend, and stand beside me, and let us show that we can resist."

Diomedes replied: "Certainly I will stand and endure the fight. Yet it seems to me that Zeus has now given his own strength to the Trojans and has determined on their victory."

So Odysseus and Diomedes stood firm and the Greeks rallied again. But Hector, looking along the ranks, saw where they stood and, shouting out his war cry, bore down on them with his picked Trojan warriors at his back. Even Diomedes shuddered as he saw great Hector in his flashing bronze. He turned to Odysseus and said: "Things look black for us two. Here comes great Hector in all his strength. We must stand firm and drive him back."

As he spoke he hurled his long-shadowed spear at Hector's head and struck him full on his helmet. The point did not pierce through the metal to the flesh, but Hector was stunned by the blow. He fell back quickly behind his men and sank to his knees, supporting himself with one strong hand on the ground, while everything went black before his eyes.

Diomedes shouted out in triumph and sprang forward, but now Paris, who had hidden himself behind the tomb of Ilus on the plain, aimed an arrow at him and shot. The arrow went through the flat part of Diomedes' foot and pinned it to the ground. Paris laughed as he came out from his ambush and cried out: "I have hit you, Diomedes, and I wish my arrow had pierced you in the lower belly, below your breastplate and robbed you of your life. Then the Trojans would have had a rest from your savagery."

Strong Diomedes replied: "You bowman, you coward, you runner after women! I wish you would stand and face me with sword and spear. As it is, you have only scratched my foot. I might have been wounded like this by a woman or a careless boy. My weapons are different. If you faced them you would soon find yourself more sought after by the vultures than by the girls."

As he spoke Odysseus came to his side and covered him with his shield. Diomedes sat down and drew the sharp arrow out of his flesh. Pain stabbed through him as he did so. His charioteer supported him to his chariot and drove him out of the battle.

And now Odysseus was left alone, since all the rest had turned in flight. "Now what," he said to himself, "will happen to me? It would be shameful to run away, yet it is a bad thing also to be caught here by myself, now that Zeus has filled the other Greeks with fear. I know however that only cowards withdraw from fighting. The brave man will stand firm and either kill or be killed."

As he deliberated thus with his own great heart the Trojan companies swarmed up to him and surrounded him, like hunters with their hounds who surround a wild boar. And as a wild boar turns from side to side with his gleaming tusks, dealing death as he charges now here now there, so Odysseus, surrounded by his enemies, fought back at them and every thrust of his spear brought wounds or death. Many were the men he killed until at length a Trojan captain (Socus was his name), with a mighty throw of his spear, pierced through the bright shield of Odysseus and tore away the flesh from his side, though Pallas Athene kept the point from any vital part. Even then Socus was afraid and turned to run; but Odysseus hurled his own spear and caught him between the shoulders, piercing his heart, so that he fell headlong to the ground in death. Then Odysseus pulled out the spear from his own wound and, as he did so, the dark blood flowed in a stream. The Trojans saw the blood and they shouted to each other and all together set upon the wounded man.

Then great Odysseus began slowly to give ground and at the same time he shouted out for help. Three times he shouted and his voice was heard by yellow-haired Menelaus, who immediately turned to Ajax and said: "I hear the voice of brave Odysseus crying for help. It must be that the Trojans have cut him off by himself in the retreat. Let us hurry to the rescue. How we would miss him, if anything happened to him!"

So the two of them charged through the Trojans and came to the place where Odysseus was still standing, with the blood pouring from his wound, keeping the Trojans at bay, though they pressed on him from all sides. Huge Ajax covered him with his shield and before his blows the Trojans gave way, while Menelaus took Odysseus by the arm and led him out of the battle to his own chariot in which they made their way back to the ships.

Meanwhile the Trojans were hurling their sharp spears at Ajax, who covered himself with his great shield and slowly gave way before them, though from time to time he would turn upon his enemies and charge, while they in their turn gave way to him, so much they feared his dauntless spirit and his strength. Stubbornly he withdrew as the shower of weapons fell upon his shield and armour. It was like when a donkey turns off the road into a field and starts to eat the crop. The boys who are in charge of him beat him with their sticks and throw stones at him, but the donkey goes on eating and, if he moves at all, he moves slowly. So Ajax retreated stubbornly from the enemy while the other Greeks were being swept over the plain by victorious Hector.

XII

THE BATTLE BY THE SHIPS

MEANWHILE ACHILLES had been watching the battle from the high stern of his black ship. He had seen the Greeks push the Trojans back almost to their city walls, and now he saw them routed and streaming back to the shelter of the trench and the wall that surrounded their ships and their camp. In the distance he saw old Nestor in his chariot and with him a wounded man. This was Machaon, son of the great healer Asclepius, a brave captain and himself an excellent doctor. Nestor had rescued him from the invincible hands of Hector and was carrying him out of the fighting to safety.

Achilles called to Patroclus and said: "Patroclus, dear friend, now I think that the Greeks will soon be begging at my knees. They are overwhelmed. But will you go now to Nestor's tent and find out who is the wounded man that he is bringing out of the battle? He looked to me like Machaon, but I could not be certain, as the horses dashed past me so quickly."

So Patroclus went along the shore to Nestor's tent. The old man himself was inside and on the table in front of him was a great silver cup which he had brought from home. It was studded with gold and had four handles on the tops of which were the figures of doves feeding. Most men could scarcely lift it when it was full, but Nestor lifted it quite easily.

Now Patroclus stood in the entrance to Nestor's tent, and the old man rose to greet him and to invite him to eat and drink. But Patroclus excused himself. "My lord Nestor," he said, "you must forgive me for not waiting. Achilles is expecting me to return to him. He sent me to inquire whether it was not Machaon whom you were bringing back in your chariot."

Nestor replied: "Indeed it was Machaon. But why is Achilles so anxious over him when our whole army is in such straits ? Agamemnon also has been wounded. So have great Diomedes and mighty Odysseus, and many others of our best and bravest. Is Achilles going to wait until we are all destroyed? I myself am an old man, yet I have taken my share in the fighting. How I wish I had the strength that I had in my youth when once I captured fifty chariots from the invaders of my country and killed their leader. And now what use to anyone is all the courage and strength of great Achilles? Later on, I am sure of it, he will weep and be ashamed when all our army is destroyed. You are his great friend. Will you not go and ask him to relent from his anger and to help us? Or let him at least allow you to take his place and lead the Myrmidons into battle. Let him give you his armour to wear. Then the Trojans would think that you were Achilles himself, and they would fall back and give us time to recover ourselves. Now too the Trojans are tired with fighting. If you led a fresh force against them you might drive them back to their city."

So Nestor spoke and Patroclus was moved by his words. He set out to run back to the tent of Achilles, but on his way he came upon another of the Greek captains, Eurypylus, limping out of the battle. He had been wounded by an arrow in the thigh and he could scarcely drag himself along. The sweat poured from his head and shoulders, and blood streamed from his wound. Patroclus went up to him to support him. His heart was full of pity for the Greeks who were dying far from their country and on whose white flesh the dogs of Troy would soon be feeding. Sadly he asked Eurypylus about the battle and Eurypylus replied: "Noble

Patroclus, there is no hope now for the Greeks. Our best men are dead or wounded. Great Hector is irresistible and the Trojans grow stronger as our men weaken. Help me, I beg you, to my ship, and tend my wound, since I know that you are skilful in this, and our own doctor, Machaon, is lying wounded himself in his tent."

"I am on my way back to Achilles," said Patroclus, "but I cannot leave you without help." And so he took Eurypylus to his tent, cut the arrow head out of the wound, washed it and put upon it healing herbs. Soon the wound began to dry and the blood ceased to flow.

Now while Patroclus was visiting Nestor and tending the wound of Eurypylus, the Greeks and Trojans fought on. In front of their trench and wall the Greeks rallied for a short time, but still Hector and his Trojans were irresistible and now the Greeks were penned inside the wall that protected their ships and the Trojans, dismounting from their horses and chariots, were forming up on foot for the assault. Paris led one of their companies and Aeneas another; but their strongest troops were under the command of Hector and of the warrior Polydamas. These were the troops whom Hector now urged on to the assault. But, just as they were about to advance to the trench, an omen appeared to them. They saw an eagle on the left, flying towards them and carrying in its claws a blood-red snake. But the snake was not dead. It writhed round in the eagle's claws and bit it in the neck, so fiercely that the eagle in pain dropped the snake down among the Trojan troops and then screamed as it made off on the currents of the air.

The Trojans shuddered when they saw the gleaming snake writhing on the ground in front of them, and Polydamas at once spoke to Hector. "Hector," he said, "you know that I am not afraid of the enemy, nor am I afraid to speak my mind, even if I happen to disagree with you. This omen was sent to us by Zeus, and it came just at the moment when we were going to advance. The eagle thought that he had the snake safe in his clutches, but he was forced to drop it and fly back to his nest in pain. So now, even if we succeed in storming the Greek wall, we too shall in the end have to retreat and shall suffer in our retreat. Therefore, I say, let us not advance today, but wait for more favourable signs."

Hector looked at him fiercely. "I tell you," he said, "that Zeus has promised me victory. You cannot put me off by your talk of the senseless doings of birds. To fight for one's country is worth all the omens in the world. Now follow me, and do not try to keep the others back, or else I shall strike you down with my own spear."

Then, shouting out to his men, Hector led the assault upon the wall. With a noise like the roaring of the sea his troops followed him, and Zeus sent out a wind which blew up the dust before them, half blinding the Greeks. Company after company swept across the trench and up to the wall.

Here indeed the Greeks fought back. They were led by huge Ajax and by his brother Teucer, the famous archer, by Idomeneus of Crete and those others of the great captains who had not been wounded. Arrows and spears fell thick among the attacking Trojans. Yet still it was impossible to hold Hector back. He picked up from the ground a great rock, pointed at one end though thick at the other, so big that nowadays it would take two men even to lift it up into a waggon. But Zeus gave Hector strength and he handled it as easily as if it were a small stone. Standing with his legs planted wide apart he hurled it at the centre of the strong bolted gate in the wall, and the blow broke the gate from its hinges, splintering the wooden panels and crashing through the bolts. The great double doors fell inwards and Hector himself, with a look on his face like black night, sprang into the breach. He held two spears in his hands and his armour shone like a star. None but a god could have withstood him as he swept through the gate. Behind him came his men, eager as wolves, and, as the Greeks fell back, still fresh parties of Trojans swarmed over the wall along its whole extent. Now the fighting was for the ships themselves and Hector, in his great voice, began to call for torches to set the ships on fire.

But now the Greeks stood firm, shoulder to shoulder in their gleaming bronze. They knew that if they were routed here they could hope for no mercy, nor would they ever be able to return to the wives and children they had left behind them in their own land. So the battle was renewed inside the wall and here the fighting was as fierce as ever it had been in the plain.

Yet still Zeus gave fresh power to Hector, for he was determined that on this day fire should be set to the Greek ships, so that he might keep the promise that he had made to Thetis, the mother of Achilles. It was only up to this point that Zeus would give Hector his aid, for in the end he had decided that the Greeks should be victorious. But now out of all those warriors Zeus was giving the greatest glory of all to Hector, since indeed he had not much longer to live and already the day of his fate was close upon him.

Now he fought like the War God himself or like a destroying fire that rages through the forests. His eyes flashed beneath his grim brows and the dreadful nodding crest of his helmet. Through the dense ranks of the Greeks he burst like a thunderbolt and forced them backwards to the first row of ships drawn up along the shore. Here once more the Greeks rallied. Great Ajax took his stand on a ship's deck, and strode from one deck to another, shouting out his commands and urging the Greeks to stand, since no further retreat was possible. In his hands he held an enormous spear of the kind that is used in sea battle and with this huge spear he kept the Trojans back. Twelve men he wounded with his spear, all eager to have the glory of being the first to set fire to the ships, and all the time, though his limbs were soaked with sweat and though spears and arrows fell in a rain upon his shield, he kept shouting to the others:

"Fight on! Fight on! The sea is behind us and our country is far away. Nothing can save us except our own right hands."

Yet there came at last a time when even Ajax had to fall back. Hector swept down upon him and with one blow of his great sword cut right through the shaft of the spear, so that Ajax, left without a weapon, had to retire from the prow of the ship where he had stood. Immediately the Trojans hurled their blazing torches into the ship and soon the flames spread over the wood and leapt up into the sky. And now indeed it seemed that irreparable disaster was facing the Greeks, and that there among their ships they would perish every one of them before the unconquerable might of Hector. Yet at this very moment the fortune of the battle was about to turn, for Patroclus was putting on the glorious armour of Achilles and making ready to lead the Myrmidons into the fight.

XIII

THE LAST FIGHT OF PATROCLUS

AT ABOUT the time that Hector was storming the wall, Patroclus had come back to the tent of Achilles. Hot tears were running down his cheeks. Swift-footed Achilles pitied him when he saw him and said: "Why are you crying, Patroclus? You look just like a little girl, running beside her mother and plucking at her dress, asking to be lifted up. Have you had bad news from home, or what is it?"

"O, Achilles," said Patroclus, "you cannot blame me for weeping. The whole army is being destroyed and already the best of the Greeks are lying wounded. Great Diomedes is out of the battle; so is Odysseus; so is Agamemnon himself, and many more. Is there nothing to be done with you, Achilles? This unending rage of yours is spoiling you. What will people say in future times, if you do nothing to help your comrades in their great need? But, if your heart is still as hard as a rock, or if you are afraid because of some prophecy from the goddess your mother, then at least allow me to lead the Myrmidons into battle. And let me wear your armour, so that at first the Trojans may take me for you. They are tired out already with fighting, and, if I joined the battle with fresh troops, I might throw them back from the ships and from the camp."

Patroclus spoke urgently to his friend, little knowing that what he was begging for was his own death. But Achilles was moved by his words. "I am certainly not afraid of any prophecies," he said. "It is simply that I will not bear the insults of Agamemnon and his ingratitude for all that I have done for him. Yet perhaps you are right and I ought not to remain angry for ever. Go, then, put on my splendid armour and lead the Myrmidons out into the battle, now that the Trojans are engulfing the Greeks like a black cloud and our friends are driven back to the edge of the sea, and the whole air rings with the shouts of manslaying Hector urging on his troops to the final assault. Take the Myrmidons, therefore, my friend, and save the ships. But you must do exactly as I tell you. When you have swept the Trojans back from the ships you must return to me here. Then the Greeks will honour me all the more. Do not chase the Trojans over the plain towards their city, or some evil may come to you from one of the immortal gods, from the Archer Apollo, perhaps, who loves the Trojans. So be sure that, once you have saved the ships, you return here to me."

As he spoke they saw in the distance the fire leaping up to the sky from the ship of Ajax. Patroclus hurried to put on the famous armour and Achilles went out of his tent to call the Myrmidons together for the fight.

Soon Patroclus was armed. He took all the weapons of Achilles except his long and heavy spear, which no Greek except Achilles himself was able to handle. This spear had been made from an ash that grew on Mount Pelion and had been given to Peleus, Achilles' father, by the good centaur Chiron, a formidable weapon that had brought death to many.

Next Patroclus called for the charioteer Automedon and told him to yoke Achilles' horses to the shining chariot. These horses, Xanthus and Balius, were a pair that flew like the wind, and indeed they were divine horses, since the West Wind was their father. Alongside these horses went Pedasus, a famous horse that Achilles had captured in the war. He was only a mortal horse but he kept up with the immortal pair.

Meanwhile Achilles had drawn up the Myrmidons in battle order. They were eager enough for the fight, as they stood there under arms, shoulder to shoulder and shield to shield. And before them went Patroclus and Automedon, each resolved to win glory by fighting in the forefront of the battle.

But Achilles went back to his tent and there he opened a beautiful chest which his mother Thetis had given him before he sailed and had filled with tunics and thick cloaks and fleecy rugs. In this chest he kept a finely-wrought drinking cup from which no one but himself was allowed to drink and from which he made his libations only to Father Zeus, using other cups when he poured out wine in prayer to the other gods.

Now Achilles washed his hands in fresh water and filled this cup with wine. Looking up at the sky as he poured the wine on the ground, he prayed: "Father Zeus, you listened to me when I prayed to you before. Now, I beg you, grant me this prayer also. My friend has gone out to battle with the Myrmidons. Give him victory, far-seeing Zeus, and strengthen his heart so that Hector may know that Patroclus can fight by himself, even when I am not with him. And when he has swept the Trojans back from the ships, let him return back to me safe and sound with his armour and with his men."

Zeus listened to the prayer of Achilles. Half of it he granted, but not the other half.

And now from between the ships the army of Myrmidons burst out upon the enemy. With a great voice Patroclus cried out to them: "Now show how you can fight, comrades of Achilles, and bring honour to him who is the best warrior among the Greeks, with the best troops under his command." So the Myrmidons, shouting their battle cry, fell upon the Trojans, swarming out upon them like wasps disturbed from their nest, who fly recklessly upon the disturbers and will not rest until they have avenged themselves.

And when the Trojans saw Patroclus in his gleaming armour with Automedon beside him, they believed that it was Achilles himself who had returned to the battle, having made up his quarrel with King Agamemnon, and every man looked round for some way of escape from the sheer destruction which threatened them. They fell back from the burning ships, and the Greeks quickly put out the flames.

Patroclus, carried behind the fleet horses of Achilles, raged among the broken Trojan ranks, killing on every side. Hector himself, experienced as he was in war, saw that the battle was lost. Leaping into his chariot he drove out over the ditch and the destroyed wall, fearing that he might be cut off before he reached the plain. There in the ditch many chariots were overturned and many men lost their lives in the headlong retreat. But Patroclus was carried by the divine horses of Achilles, and they easily leapt over the ditch and hurried forward in pursuit of Hector, for it was against Hector most of all that Patroclus yearned to fight. But Hector's horses also were fast and they carried him out of danger. The full fury of Patroclus turned upon the Lycians, allies of the Trojans, who fought under the command of their king Sarpedon, whose father was Zeus himself and whose mother was the daughter of the great hero Bellerophon. Sarpedon had been the first to climb the Greek wall, when Hector broke through the gate, and all day he, with his friend Glaucus, had fought in the front ranks. Glaucus indeed had been wounded by the great archer Teucer, the brother of Ajax, in the fight by the ships, but he remained still with his troops, encouraging them to battle. Sarpedon had killed many men that day, and now, when he saw his Lycian troops being driven in disorder before Patroclus, he cried out to them to stand firm. "Let me see myself," he said, "what sort of man this is who has done such harm to the Trojans this day." And he leapt down from his chariot, advancing towards Patroclus on foot. Patroclus too jumped down from his chariot and came to meet him, brandishing his huge spear. Just as two crook-clawed vultures scream and fight together on the top of a rocky cliff, so these two came together in battle and neither of them would yield.

All day Zeus, from his heavenly seat, had kept his eyes fixed on the fighting. Now he sighed deeply and said: "Alas! Now I know that it is fated for Sarpedon, whom I love most of all men, to die at the hands of Patroclus. Yet I will save his body and set it down in the rich land of Lycia, far from this lamentable battle, where his friends will give him burial." Then Zeus, in honour to his son, sent down to the earth drops of blood falling like rain.

Now Patroclus hurled his first spear and struck down dead the charioteer who stood at King Sarpedon's side. Sarpedon cast next and missed Patroclus with his spear; but he struck the horse Pedasus in the right shoulder and the horse collapsed in the dust and, heaving a great sigh, breathed out its life. The other two horses reared up and sprang apart, entangling the reins; but Automedon quickly cut the thongs of the harness, separating the immortal pair from the dead horse who had been their stable companion.

Sarpedon once more hurled a spear but the point flew over Patroclus's left shoulder. And now Patroclus forced his own spear home. It struck Sarpedon in the upper part of the stomach near the heart, and he fell with a crash like an oak falls or a high-standing pine which woodmen have cut down in the mountains. He clutched at the wound with his hands, and all the ground was wet with his blood. Breathing his last, he cried out: "Dear Glaucus, now is the time to show your courage and your strength. Fight for me now, and save my body from the Greeks." As he spoke, his life left him.

Pain and grief filled the heart of Glaucus as he heard the words of his dying friend. He clutched his wounded arm which was too weak to hold a spear and he prayed to the Archer God Apollo. "Hear me," he said, "Lord of the Silver Bow! Our best man is dead and I am powerless to defend his body. Even Zeus has not helped his own son.

Heal my wound, therefore, I pray you, that I may at least fight for him now that he is dead."

Apollo heard the prayer of Glaucus and immediately the blood dried and the pain departed from his wound. And now both Trojans and Lycians joined in the fight for the body of Sarpedon. Hector himself stood at Glaucus' side. Shame and anger filled his heart at the thought of the death of his great ally. But Patroclus still raged forward and with him was towering Ajax and all the companies of the Myrmidons.

For long they fought together, and Zeus, looking down on the battle, was in two minds whether he should now allow Patroclus to be slain at the hands of Hector, or whether he should let him live a little longer, so that he should do more harm still to the Trojans. He decided that for a short time he would let him live. Then gradually the Greeks pushed back the Lycians and the Trojans from the body of Sarpedon. They stripped off the splendid armour and would have taken the body also, but Zeus surrounded the body with a mist, and Apollo lightly took it up into the air away from the battle. He washed the wounds with water and anointed them with ambrosia. Then he dressed the body of great Sarpedon in imperishable garments and set it down in the rich land of Lycia, far away from the fighting.

And now both Trojans and Lycians turned in flight. Patroclus, shouting his war-cry, drove his swift horses in pursuit. Zeus had made him over-daring; for, if he had remembered the orders of Achilles, he might now have returned safely and with honour to his friend. As it was he drove the Trojans before him right up to the walls of Troy, and, in his pride, he determined that on that very day he himself would capture the city. But this was not the will of the immortal gods, and the city was guarded by Apollo himself.

Three times Patroclus climbed up to the wall, and three times Apollo thrust him back. Still Patroclus came on, raging like a demon, and then the god spoke to him with a terrible voice: "Go back, Patroclus! It is not fated that Troy should be captured by your spear, and not even by the spear of Achilles, who is a far better man than you."

Then Patroclus retired for a little from the wall, but still he was determined to go on killing the Trojans till night fell, and most of all he desired to fight with Hector. Again and again he charged into the battle like a savage lion. Man after man fell before his spear and now he surely thought that he was invincible. Yet it was not only against men that he had to fight, for the god Apollo was protecting the Trojans. Wrapped round in a mist he came in all his strength and terror and met Patroclus in the very thick of the fighting. Standing behind him, he struck him between the shoulders with the flat of his hand; he broke his great spear in fragments and hurled from his head the shining helmet to roll among the horses' hooves. Never before had this helmet, which used to cover the glorious head of Achilles, been seen to fall in the dust; but now Zeus allowed Hector to wear it for a short time, since his own death was very close. As for Patroclus, darkness swam before his eyes; stunned and dazed, he staggered backwards, and his legs, as in a dream, seemed to have lost their strength to carry him. And now Hector thrust at him with his spear, striking him in the lower part of the stomach, where death comes quickest. His body crashed to the ground, and Hector exulted over him. "Patroclus," he cried, "you thought that you would destroy my city, and sell the Trojan women into slavery. But all the time I, Hector, was there to protect them, and now the vultures are going to feed upon your body. Not Achilles himself could save you from my spear."

In a feeble voice Patroclus replied to him from the ground where he lay bleeding. "You can boast now, Hector," he said, "since Zeus and Apollo have given you the victory. It was they who conquered me. As for you, I would not have shrunk back if twenty Hectors had come against me.

And now listen to my words. I tell you that you too have not long to live. Strong destiny is drawing near to you, and death at the hands of Achilles."

As he spoke death closed Patroclus' eyes; his soul sped out of his limbs and went down to Hades, lamenting its fate, leaving behind its manhood and its youth.

XIV

ACHILLES AND PATROCLUS

WHEN PATROCLUS died the Greeks shuddered, and their whole army fell back. Quickly Hector stripped the body of its splendid armour, the armour of Achilles which the gods had given to his father Peleus, and Peleus in his old age had given to his son when he set out for Troy. This armour Hector put upon his own body, and was to wear it for a little time. So he stood resplendent among the Trojans and their allies. His heart yearned for battle and the gods put fresh courage in his spirit, fresh strength into his limbs. Shouting to his men, he charged forward, and first of all he determined to capture the divine horses of Achilles and his shining chariot.

Now these horses, ever since they had seen Patroclus fall in the dust, had stood still, with the tears streaming from their eyes. Automedon, their charioteer, had done all he could to make them move, using his whip, speaking to them softly and cursing at them; but they stayed stock-still, like a statue over the grave of a dead man; their heads were bowed to the earth; the hot tears fell from their eyes as they grieved for Patroclus, and their silky manes were draggled in the dust.

Zeus, looking down upon the battle, saw the two horses and pitied them. "Poor creatures!" he said to himself, "why did we give you to King Peleus, who is a mortal, you who are ageless and immortal? Why should you share in the sorrows of wretched men? For man is the most miserable

of all things that breathe and go upon the earth. Now
certainly I shall not allow you to fall into Hector's hands.
Already he has the armour and still I am giving him glory
in the battle. For I intend him to drive the Greeks over the
plain until the sun sets and darkness comes down upon the
earth."

So Zeus put strength into the horses' legs, and they flew
off, fast as the wind.

And now Hector turned to the body of Patroclus. He
wished to drag it away, to cut off the head and leave the
flesh to be devoured by the jackals. But the Greeks had
rallied. Huge Ajax stood like a tower, covering the body of
Patroclus with his shield. At his side was yellow-haired
Menelaus and the great warrior Meriones. More and more
entered the fight. They made a wall of their shields, and
not even Hector could break through the wall. And now
Ajax sent a messenger to the Prince Antilochus, the son of
Nestor, who was fighting at the other end of the battle line.
When the messenger found him, he said: "Antilochus, I
have terrible news to tell. I wish that it had never happened.
Patroclus has been killed and our whole army will feel the
lack of him. And now Ajax bids you to hurry to Achilles
and tell him that his dear friend is dead. Tell him that we
are struggling to bring his body back to the ships—just his
naked body, since Hector has stripped it of its glorious
armour."

When Antilochus heard the news, the tears stood in his
eyes and for long he was unable to speak. Yet he did as he
was asked to do and ran back towards the ships with bitter
tidings for Achilles.

Now spear was locked with spear and shield with shield
over the body of Patroclus.

Yet still the Trojan powers increased. Hector, Aeneas
and Glaucus fought as they had never fought before. From
Mount Ida Zeus sent lightning flashes down upon the
plain, clearly revealing that now he was giving victory to

the Trojans. Even Ajax was appalled, and at his advice
Menelaus and Meriones took the body of Patroclus and
began to withdraw with it towards the ships, while Ajax himself rallied the Greeks and covered their retreat. Thick mist
overhung that part of the field where the fighting raged
over Patroclus, though in other parts it was bright sunshine.

Menelaus and Meriones lifted the body in their arms and
came with it out of the mist. On all sides they saw the
Trojans advancing and they made what haste they could,
fearing that they might be cut off. Behind them was the
furious din of men and horses in battle. Man after man the
Greeks were falling before the spears of Hector and of
Aeneas. They scattered and cried out like a flock of jack-
daws or starlings when a hawk bears down upon them. So
they forgot their courage and were pressed back again to
the ditch, and still the fury of their enemies increased.

Meanwhile Antilochus had reached the ships and come
to Achilles with his bitter news. He found Achilles standing
in front of his black ship and already his heart was distressed.
"Why is it," he was saying to himself, "that the long-haired
Greeks are once more being chased back over the plain?
What can have happened? I dread lest my mother's prophecy may be fulfilled; for once she told me that, while I
was still alive, the best of the Myrmidons would be killed.
Oh, is Patroclus dead? Could he not obey me when I told
him to come back here and not to fight with Hector?"

And now Antilochus stood before Achilles, with the hot
tears pouring from his eyes. "Alas, Achilles," he said, "I
have terrible news for you. Patroclus is killed and they are
fighting round his naked body. Hector has stripped him of
your armour."

As he spoke, the black darkness of unspeakable pain came
upon Achilles. In his two hands he picked up the dark dust
and poured it over his head and over his beautiful face.
Then he threw himself on the ground and lay there, with
his fine body stretched out, like a great statue fallen, and he

tore his hair in his misery, while the women servants, girls whom he and Patroclus had captured, came out to him and, when they saw him, they wailed and beat their breasts. Antilochus, with the tears still falling from his eyes, sat down beside him and held his hands, since he feared that now, while he was sobbing his heart out, he might snatch a sword and make away with himself. Then Achilles cried out aloud with a dreadful cry, and his mother Thetis heard him in the place where she was sitting in the depths of the sea, with her sisters, the Nereids, beautiful goddesses of the sea, around her. At the sound of her son's voice she also cried aloud and she said to her sisters: "Oh, unhappy that I am! Unhappy to be the mother of the best and greatest of all men! I nursed him like a tender shoot in the corner of a walled garden; but he went to fight at Troy and I shall never welcome him returning home to the house of Peleus. Even his short life is filled with sorrow, and I can do nothing to help him. Yet I will go to him and find out what new grief this is that he has suffered."

So she left the deep sea cave and her sisters came with her through the surging waters of the sea. One by one they came up on to the beach where the ships of the Myrmidons were. Thetis stood by Achilles and gently spoke to him, "Dear child, why are you crying? Has not Zeus done for you as I prayed him? For now, fighting without you, the Greeks are being driven back to their ships."

Achilles groaned as he answered her. "Mother," he said, "it is true that Zeus has fulfilled my prayer. But what joy can I have in it? Patroclus is killed, the friend whom I honoured more than all others and loved like my own life. I have lost him, and Hector has taken the glorious armour that the gods gave to Peleus when you were married to him, a mortal. Now there is no will to live in my heart. I would rather die. Only first I desire to strike down Hector with my spear, and avenge the death of my comrade."

His mother wept as she listened to him. "My child," she

said, "what you are saying is bringing on your own death; for in no long time after the death of Hector you too are fated to die."

"Then let death come quickly," said Achilles, "since I was not there to help my friend in his greatest need. Instead I was sitting here by my ships, a useless burden on the earth. But now I will go and find Hector, the slayer of my friend. After that I shall take whatever fate is sent me by Zeus and by the other immortal gods."

Then Thetis, the silver-footed goddess, answered him. "I know," she said, "that I cannot make you alter your mind. But now Hector is wearing your beautiful armour and you have no weapons with which to fight. Stay here till tomorrow's dawn, and then I will come back to you and bring you immortal armour which the god Hephaestus will make for me."

So saying she left him. Her sisters, the Nereids, went back into the depths of the sea, but Thetis sped through the air to Olympus in order to ask the craftsman of the gods to make armour for her son.

Meanwhile the Greeks were fleeing before Hector over the plain, and now it seemed doubtful indeed whether they would succeed in saving the body of Patroclus from the rage of his enemies. Three times Hector laid hold of the feet as he tried to drag it away, and each time great Ajax pushed him back again. But still Hector came on like a hungry lion whom shepherds try to drive from the body of a sheep or bullock, and certainly he would have seized the body and taken it back to Troy, if Zeus had not willed otherwise. He sent his messenger Iris to Achilles and told him to show himself, unarmed as he was, outside the wall. So Achilles rose from the ground where he was lying and over his shoulders the goddess Athene threw her own terrible aegis; she put a golden mist around his head and from the mist she sent out piercing beams of light. Achilles stood by the trench and shouted aloud his tremendous war cry. Athene cried out too, and the sound of those terrible cries was like the sounds of trumpets calling to the assault. The Trojans fell back in turn; their long-maned horses twisted round in the shafts and began to pull the chariots back; the charioteers trembled when they saw that awful light blazing from the head of Achilles. Three times Achilles let his cry ring out over the plain, and three times there was tumult and confusion in the Trojan ranks. And now Hera caused the sun to set. Night put an end to the battle and thus the Greeks were saved. They brought the body of Patroclus over the trench and laid it down on a stretcher. Hot tears fell from the eyes of Achilles when he saw the body of his faithful friend so terribly wounded by the sharp spear of Hector. He laid his man-slaying hands on his comrade's breast and he groaned aloud, like a bearded lion when a hunter has killed one of his cubs and he comes too late to save it. "Ah, Patroclus," he said, "I promised your father that I would bring you back safe and famous from Troy, rich with the riches that we would win there. But Zeus will not grant all our prayers. Now it is fated that both you and I must make the same earth red with our blood, here in the land of Troy; for I too shall never return home to my father and my mother. I, Patroclus, shall follow you beneath the earth; and so I shall not give you burial until I have brought here the arms and the head of Hector, who killed you. And on your tomb I shall sacrifice twelve young men, all Trojan nobles, to do you honour. Meanwhile the Trojan women whom we captured together shall wail for you day and night, and you shall lie here in honour by my ships."

Then he ordered his servants to put a great cauldron on the fire to heat water for the washing of the body. When the water was hot they washed the dead limbs and put ointment in the wounds. They laid the body on a bed and put a soft sheet over it from head to foot; over that they stretched a white cloak. And so throughout the night Achilles and the Myrmidons mourned for Patroclus.

XV

ACHILLES PREPARES FOR BATTLE

B̲ᴜᴛ ɴᴏ sooner had Dawn risen from the stream of
Ocean, than the goddess, silver-footed Thetis, came
to Achilles with wonderful armour made for him by
the gods. She had been to Olympus, to the bright gleaming
house of the lame god Hephaestus. There she had found
him with sweat streaming down over his shaggy breast, as
he hurried to and fro, tending his fires and blowing them to
intense heat with his gigantic bellows. He made all the
furniture for the houses of the gods, and now he was busy
with some beautiful banqueting tables with golden wheels.

When he saw that the goddess had come to visit him, he
collected the tools that he had been using and put them away
in a silver box. Then he washed his hands and sponged his
face and neck and shaggy chest. He put on his tunic, took
his sceptre in his hand and went limping out to meet her.
He had miraculous servants who attended on him. They
were made of gold, but they looked exactly like real women,
and could even speak and obey his orders and do all the
work that women do. With these golden creatures to wait
upon him, he sat down with Thetis and asked her what she
needed from him.

Once more the goddess wept as she told him of her son's
distress and of how he had begged her to find him armour,
now that Hector wore the splendid arms of Peleus.

Hephaestus immediately agreed to help her. He went back
to his workshop, took hammer and tongs in his hand and

prepared the metals he needed for his work—bronze, tin, silver and shining gold. First he made a wonderful shield, strong enough to resist all weapons, five layers thick and decorated with all kinds of designs. On this great shield were engraved the sun and moon and the constellations, cities of men too, vineyards, minstrels and dancers. It was a wonder to see, and it seemed to give out its own light. Then the god made a breastplate which shone brighter than the gleam of fire. He made a strong helmet with a golden crest, and greaves of tin that fitted well over the ankles and round the legs.

This was the splendid armour that he gave to Thetis. Gratefully she took it from him and swooped down with it like a hawk from snowy Olympus.

She found her son by the ships, still weeping for Patroclus and clasping the dead body in his arms. Taking his hand gently, she said to him: "My child, he was killed by the will of the gods, and we must suffer it to be so, however much we may grieve. Now you must take this armour. It is altogether marvellous and such as no man has ever yet worn upon his shoulders."

So saying, she put the armour down in front of him, and it rang upon the ground. All the Myrmidons trembled when they saw it; they turned pale and scarcely dared to set their eyes upon it. But the more Achilles looked, the more he felt the anger rising in his heart; beneath his brows his eyes flashed like fire; carefully and with deep delight he handled the wonderful gifts of Hephaestus. "Mother," he said, "this is certainly the work of a god. No mortal could have made such arms. And now I shall make ready for battle. But I am afraid that the flies may come and settle in the wounds of Patroclus and that his body will begin to rot."

"Do not fear," said Thetis, "I shall see that his body remains fresh and pure. I shall put nectar and ambrosia upon his flesh and will make it incorruptible. But now you must call the Greeks to an assembly and make peace with

Agamemnon. Afterwards prepare for battle, and I will fill you with unconquerable strength."

Then Thetis put nectar and ambrosia upon the body of Patroclus, and Achilles rose and went along the shore of the sea, shouting out to the Greeks to call them to the assembly. Quickly they came together, and among them came great Diomedes and wise Odysseus, both limping from their wounds and supporting themselves on their spears. Last of all came Agamemnon, and he too was still suffering from the wound that he had received from the spear of Coön, Antenor's son.

When all the Greeks were gathered together, Achilles rose and spoke. "King Agamemnon," he said, "I wish that you and I had never quarrelled for the sake of that girl. Only Hector and the Trojans have profited by it, and as a result of it many of the Greeks now lie dead. What is done cannot be undone, but for the future my anger is at an end. I propose that now you call the Greeks to battle. I shall be fighting with them, and I think that the Trojans will be more anxious to run away than to face my spear in stubborn war."

The Greeks cried out with joy when they heard this speech of Achilles. Then Agamemnon rose and, turning to Achilles, said: "Indeed I have myself cursed the day when I was so blinded by anger that I took away your prize and caused this feud between us. It was not I, I think, but Zeus and Fate and the Furies that caused the quarrel. Now I too relinquish my anger. Arm yourself, great Achilles, and lead the Greeks into battle. And it is still my desire to give you all those gifts which yesterday Odysseus promised you in my name. I will send them to you now, if you wish it so."

Achilles replied to him: "I thank you, King Agamemnon. As for the gifts, you may give them to me, if you think it right, or keep them. But now I cannot wait before joining in the battle. All delay is hateful to me until I am cutting down the Trojan companies with my spear. I want neither food nor drink until our losses have been avenged."

And with this he would have led the Greeks immediately into battle, so eager was he to avenge the death of his friend, and to be surrounded with blood and slaughter and the thick breathing of dying men. But now Odysseus rose and said: "Great Achilles, you are a stronger man than I am and better with your spear. All the same I have more experience than you have, and it is my advice that should be taken. There is a day's fighting in front of our troops and they cannot be expected to fight well on empty stomachs. Certainly we must mourn for our dead, but not by fasting, if there is fighting to be done afterwards. Therefore let every man first prepare his meal and meanwhile let the gifts be brought to Achilles' tent. Then we will sacrifice a boar to Zeus and to the Sun. After that let no one be found lingering by the ships. We will go into battle with every single man who can bear arms."

Though he still yearned to plunge immediately into the war, Achilles recognised the wisdom of what Odysseus said. He returned to his tent and there the Greek kings and chieftains attended him to make ready the sacrifice. Meanwhile the heralds of Agamemnon brought the gifts which he had promised. The lady Briseis came too, as beautiful as golden Aphrodite. When she saw the body of Patroclus with its deep wounds, she cried aloud and flung herself down beside the corpse. "Oh Patroclus," she cried, "you were alive when I went away and now, returning, I find you dead. So it is with me always—one suffering after another. I saw my husband, my father and my three brothers all killed before my eyes. Yet you were always kind to me. You told me not to cry. You told me that you would take me back with you and make me the lawful wife of Achilles, and give me a great wedding feast among the Myrmidons. Always you were gentle and kind to me, and always I shall weep for you."

So Briseis lamented, and the other women lamented with her. Some indeed were weeping for Patroclus, but others were in reality weeping for their own sad state as captives who had lost their fathers and their brothers and their husbands in the war.

The leaders of the Greeks, Agamemnon and Menelaus, Odysseus and Nestor, all urged Achilles to take some food before entering the battle, but he still refused. "My dear friends," he said, "my grief is too great. Do not, I beg you, ask me to eat or drink until today's sun sets."

So he waited, still mourning for his friend, while the others took their meal, and then, when the time came for the troops to muster, he began to put on his splendid armour. He fitted the greaves carefully to his legs; he put on the shining breastplate and slung over his shoulder the great bronze sword with silver-studded hilt. Then he took up the enormous shield which flashed out like a beacon light which sailors see burning on a headland in the dusk. He fitted the helmet on his head, and it shone out like a star. And all the time that he was arming himself his devouring anger burnt within his heart. He gnashed his teeth and his eyes flashed terribly beneath his brows. Finally he took the great ashen spear of Peleus which he alone could handle. Already his horses were harnessed and yoked to the chariot, and Automedon, the charioteer, had taken the reins in his hand. Achilles, shining like the sun, stepped into the chariot and, looking down at his divine horses, shouted to them fiercely: "Xanthus and Balius, my famous horses, this time repay the care that has been given to you. Bring back your master safe from the battle and do not leave him there dead, as you left Patroclus."

Then from under the yoke one of the swift horses answered him. It was Xanthus to whom the white-armed goddess Hera had given the power of speech. Xanthus lowered his head, trailing his long mane on the ground. "Great Achilles," he said, "we shall indeed bring you safely back again today. But the day of your death is drawing near. Nor must you blame us for being the cause of it, since it will come to you from powerful Fate and from the hands of a great god. And it was not because we were slow or unwilling that Patroclus died. Great Apollo destroyed him and gave the glory to Hector. So though we run with the speed of the West Wind, you also are fated to lose your life in battle with a god and with a man."

As he spoke the Furies cut short his words. Achilles answered him angrily. "Xanthus," he said, "there is no need for you to prophesy my death. I know well enough myself that I am doomed to die here, far from my father and my mother. Yet there is nothing in the world that can keep me from the war."

So saying he shouted to his men and drove the horses forward to the fighting.

XVI

THE ROUT OF THE TROJANS

MEANWHILE HECTOR and Aeneas had drawn up their army in the plain. Once more Hector's comrade, the wise Polydamas, had given good advice, but his advice had not been taken. Polydamas had spoken to the leaders of the Trojans and said: "It is true that we have won victories in the time that Achilles took no part in the war. But now his quarrel with King Agamemnon is over and he is angry for the death of his friend. I fear that when he leads his Myrmidons into battle we shall lose many more men than we lost at the hands of Patroclus. My advice therefore is that we should retreat to the city and defend ourselves there behind our walls."

To this Hector had replied: "Polydamas, is this the time to talk of retreat, now when the gods have given us such a victory and when we have forced our enemies back upon their ships? Run away, if you like; but you will not find any Trojans to follow you. As for Achilles, if he really has decided to fight, he may well be sorry for it. I shall not run away from him, but shall meet him face to face. No victory is certain, and in war the man who expects to kill is often killed himself."

The Trojans had shouted out in favour of Hector and against Polydamas. Pallas Athene had taken away their wits.

Now they stood ready for battle in the plain and now Zeus summoned the blessed gods to Olympus. "Today," he said to them, "will be fought the greatest battle of the war, and today you may join in the fighting, each on the side which you prefer. For if Achilles were to fight alone in his anger, nothing could withstand him and he would take the high walls of Troy before the time that is fated."

So the immortal gods themselves went to war. On the side of the Greeks were Hera and Athene and Poseidon, the Earth-shaker. Strong Hephaestus went with them and Hermes, the Giver of Good Luck. On the side of the Trojans were Ares, the god of War, Phoebus Apollo and his sister Artemis, Leto, the great river god Xanthus and laughter-loving Aphrodite.

And now the blessed gods hurled the two armies together in battle. From heaven there rang out the terrible thunder of Zeus and Poseidon shook the earth. The woods and high crests of Ida trembled; the great walls of Troy quaked and the masts of the Greek ships were shaken like reeds. Down in the lower world the dreadful King of the Dead cried out in terror and leapt up from his throne; for he feared that Poseidon would split the earth open above his head and let light in among the terrible dwelling places of the Dead, those vast decaying mansions where the ghosts flit to and fro and which are hated by the gods themselves.

So the armies rushed together and on each side the gods put courage and resolution into the hearts of their favourites. Achilles, flaming in his armour, searched in the battle line for Hector. It was Hector above all men that he longed to meet with. Yet the first to meet him from the Trojan ranks was Prince Aeneas, whose heart had been filled with courage by Apollo, so that he dared to stand out in front of the army to challenge Achilles with his spear. Achilles sprang to meet him, but first he cried out: "Aeneas, how is it that you have found the courage to face me, man to man? Have Priam and the Trojans offered you great rewards, waving fields of corn and vineyards, if you kill me? I think you will find that hard to do, and I advise you to turn back among your troops for safety, before safety is beyond your reach."

"Achilles," replied Aeneas, "do not imagine that you will frighten me with words as though I was a child. I know that you are a great warrior and that you are the son of a goddess, silver-footed Thetis. I also have a goddess for my mother and she is golden Aphrodite. One of these two today will mourn for her son. As for strength in war, Zeus gives it to a man or withholds it, since he rules over everything. Cease fighting with words, then, and let our bronze spears decide between us."

As he finished speaking he raised his great spear and hurled it at Achilles' shield. The metal rang out as the point struck it, and Achilles feared that the spear would pierce clean through to his body. He had forgotten that the handiwork of the gods is not so easily pierced by mortal strength. Through two of the layers that Hephaestus had made the spear passed, but there were three layers more and on the third layer the point was blunted and the ashen spear fell to the ground.

Next Achilles hurled his spear. It caught the shield of Aeneas at the thinnest part, near the edge, and went right through. Aeneas sank down, pushing the shield upwards above his head, and the great spear passed over his back and stuck in the ground. But it had come so close to him that he stood still for a moment with his eyes darkened in terror. Now Achilles had drawn his sword and with a tremendous shout, sprang towards him. Aeneas lifted up a huge rock, so big that it would have taken two men, such as men are today, even to raise it from the ground. But Aeneas handled it easily by himself. With it he would have hit the helmet or the shield of Achilles, and then Achilles would have been upon him with his sword; but the gods were watching the battle and now Poseidon, the Earth-shaker, exclaimed: "Though I favour the Greeks, I cannot bear to see the good Aeneas killed by great Achilles. Zeus himself would be angry at this, for Aeneas is destined to survive the war and to restore the fortunes of Troy in another country. He and his children after him will be great kings."

So Poseidon swept into the battle. He threw a mist over Achilles' eyes and picked up his spear from the ground, laying it down at his feet. Then he took hold of Aeneas and raised him lightly in the air, carrying him over the ranks of men, the chariots and the horses, and setting him down at the far end of the battlefield where the troops were on the point of going into action. Then he said to him: "Aeneas, it is madness for you to fight against Achilles. He is stronger than you and dearer to the immortal gods. If you see him anywhere in the fighting, avoid him. But once he is dead, you need have no fear, since no other Greek has the power to take your life."

Meanwhile the mist had fallen from Achilles' eyes and he looked about him in astonishment, finding his own spear at his feet and Aeneas vanished. "Indeed," he said to himself, "Aeneas must be dear to the immortal gods, who have saved him from my spear. Let him go. There are others who will not be saved."

Then, calling to his men, he plunged into the battle. On the other side Hector was encouraging the Trojans. "Do not be afraid of Achilles," he shouted to them. "Strong though he is, the gods do not always give victory to mere strength. As for me I shall certainly face him man to man, even though his hands are like fire and his spirit like shining steel."

Then he shouted out his war cry, but Apollo stood beside him and said: "Hector, do not by any means go and fight single-handed with Achilles. Stay in the ranks with the others and let him find you there." So Hector, obeying the voice of the god, went back into the ranks of men.

But there was nothing to hold back Achilles. With the first blow of his spear he split a man's skull in two. Next he killed one of Antenor's sons, shattering his helmet to pieces with his spear. And then he encountered Polydorus who was the youngest of Priam's sons and whom his father had forbidden to join in the fighting. But Polydorus was quick upon his feet and was showing his speed proudly as he rushed backwards and forwards among the fighters in the front line. Achilles however was a faster runner than any man alive. He swept down upon the young man and thrust his spear through his body. Polydorus fell dying to the ground, clutching the bloody wound with his hands.

When Hector saw his brother dying in agony, the tears came to his eyes and he could no longer bear to hold himself back. Brandishing his spear, he rushed at Achilles like a burning fire. Achilles sprang forward to meet him, joyfully finding at last the man who had killed his dear friend. Looking grimly on him from beneath his brows, he said: "Come quickly, for now your fate is upon you."

"Achilles," said Hector, "you need not try to frighten me with words. I know that you are the stronger man, but these things lie upon the knees of the gods. Though I am not so strong, they may allow me to kill you with my spear. It has been found sharp enough before now."

With these words he hurled his spear, but Athene was watching over Achilles. As with a breath of air she turned the spear aside and caused it to lose all its force, so that it fell at Hector's feet. Achilles rushed forward in his passion to kill; but the god Apollo, easily, as is the way of gods, hid Hector in a mist and bore him away.

Three times Achilles charged, thrusting with his spear at the empty mist. Then he cried out: "Hector, you dog, once more you have escaped me, though death was close upon you. But we shall meet once more, and then perhaps I too shall have a god to help me."

So saying he plunged once more into the fight and man after man fell before his sword and before his spear. He raged among the Trojans like a whirling wind that drives the flames this way and that when there is a forest fire along the dry slopes of the mountains. The earth ran black with blood; the hooves of his horses trampled over dead bodies and broken shields; the chariot wheels and the rails of the chariot dripped with blood as Achilles swept forward over the plain, dealing death on every side with his unconquerable hands.

The Trojan army turned in flight and was driven back to the ford of the eddying river Scamander, which the gods call Xanthus. Here Achilles cut the army into two. One part fled over the plain towards the city, while the other part was huddled together in a bend of the great river. These tried to escape by swimming, throwing away their armour and their shields, but still Achilles chased them into the river stream. Leaving his spear on the bank he went into the water with his sword and there he mercilessly destroyed these unarmed men as they cowered under the steep banks. The water ran red with their blood and all the air was filled with their crying and their groans.

Here, among many others, he killed Lycaon, a son of Priam. When first Lycaon saw him he ran to him and fell upon his knees, begging for mercy and promising a great ransom for his life. Achilles looked at him grimly and said: "Do not talk to me of mercy. Before Patroclus was killed I used to take prisoners and to accept ransom; but now not a single Trojan who falls into my power will escape with his life. No, my friend, you too must die. And why should you so complain? Patroclus died, and he was a better man than you by far. Consider me also, strong and beautiful as I am, the son of a great hero and with a goddess for my mother. Yet over me too hangs the stern necessity of death. Most surely there will be a morning or an evening or a noon when someone will take my life in battle, either with a thrust of the spear or with an arrow from the bow."

Still Lycaon knelt before him, hopelessly stretching out his hands; but Achilles struck him on the neck with his sword, burying the blade in the flesh. Out spurted the dark blood as Lycaon fell on his face. Achilles took the body by the foot and hurled it into the stream. "Lie there," he said, "and let the fish lick the blood from your wound. So may you all perish! Not the river himself can save you, nor shall I rest from slaughter till I have choked his silver streams with corpses."

Once more he sprang upon the Trojans, but now Xanthus, the god of the river, rose in anger. His voice came from the depths of the water and he said: "Achilles, you have shed too much blood already. My lovely streams are stained with it, and so many are the bodies that I can scarcely roll my river to the sea. Put an end now to the slaughter and leave me. I am horrified by your deeds."

"Great Scamander," said Achilles, "it shall be so, but not yet. I shall not cease killing until I have met with Hector face to face."

Again he plunged into the river, but now the god drew together all his streams and hurled himself upon Achilles. Roaring like a bull, he threw out on to the land all the dead bodies that Achilles had slain; then, arching himself up into a great wave, he bore down upon Achilles himself, falling with such weight upon his shield that Achilles could no longer stand upright. He seized hold of a strong elm tree to support himself, but the tree came out by the roots, tearing a great gap in the river bank. Then Achilles sprang on to the land and began to run, but still the river rose and followed him in a great wave arching black above his shoulders, roaring in anger as it sped in pursuit. Though Achilles was the greatest runner alive, the gods are more powerful than men and still the river gained upon him. Sometimes he would attempt to stand against the flood, but then the great wave would batter him to his knees, and, as he struggled up, the flowing water would circle his knees and wash the ground from beneath his feet. And now Achilles groaned as he looked up into the broad sky. "O Father Zeus," he cried, "will no god pity me and save me from the river? Indeed I would rather have been killed at the hands of Hector. He is the best man in Troy, and it would be no dishonour to die in fair fight with him. But now I am dying an unmanly death, caught up in a great stream of water."

But the gods were not unmindful of Achilles. Athene came to him and said: "Have no fear, Achilles. You are not fated to die by the river. The gods are on your side and soon the river will sink down again. As for you, do not rest from the fighting until you have driven the Trojans to their walls and taken the life of Hector."

As she spoke she put new strength into Achilles' limbs and he struggled forward through the flooded plain and the whirling waters where arms and dead bodies, branches of trees and the wreckage of chariots jostled together in the flood. Still the god of the river followed in pursuit, but now Hera called to her son Hephaestus, the God of Fire, and said to him "Quick, my son! Bring fire upon the plain and drive Xanthus back! Burn the trees along his bank and scorch his waters with your consuming flames!"

Hephaestus was quick to obey. Running fire spread over the level ground, burning up the corpses and the arms. Fire blazed from the tree tops along the river bank. Down in the deep pools the eels and the fishes darting about in their cool homes felt the scorching blaze of the breath of Hephaestus. Soon the waters boiled and steamed and began to shrink away.

Then Xanthus cried out for mercy. "Put out your fires, Hephaestus!" he said. "I cannot stand against you. Give me peace now and I swear that I will help the Trojans no more, not even on the day when all their towers are swallowed up in the fires that the Greeks will make."

So, at his mother's bidding, Hephaestus withdrew his burning flames. Now the plain was dry as dust and the winding river flowed again in its usual channel.

Achilles gathered himself together, gripped his great spear in his hand and set out once more in pursuit of the Trojans who were fleeing to the shelter of their city.

XVII

THE DEATH OF HECTOR

OLD PRIAM was standing on the city walls. In the distance he saw the Trojan army fleeing in terror before the savage might of Achilles and the Greeks who followed him. With a deep groan he went down to the gates and ordered the watchmen to set them wide open and to be ready to close them again quickly when the routed army had reached safety lest Achilles himself should burst in after them and massacre the Trojans in their own streets. And indeed this is what Achilles would have done, had it not been for Apollo who put on the shape of a Trojan prince who was fleeing from Achilles' spear. Achilles sped after him, but always the god kept a little way in front and Achilles wondered at the strange speed of foot that could outdistance him. So Apollo drew him away from the mass of the Trojans who poured back into their city and found safety there. They wiped the sweat from their bodies and refreshed themselves with drink, leaning against the beautiful battlements, while the main Greek army, with shields slung over their shoulders, approached the gates. But dark fate kept Hector outside the town, standing in front of the Scaean Gate alone.

And now Apollo spoke to Achilles and said: "Why do you pursue me, Achilles? However fast you run, you will never overtake me; for you are a mortal and I am a god. Now look back and you will see that the Trojans have escaped you."

Achilles spoke to him in anger. "Deceitful god," he said, "be sure that I would pay you back for this if I had the power. Had it not been for you I might have stormed the walls of Troy this very day."

And, turning away from him, he began to run back again towards the city, striding easily like a powerful racehorse that has outdistanced the others and confidently finishes the course.

Old Priam was the first to see him as he came running over the plain with his burnished armour, shining like a star. When the old man saw him, he groaned aloud and called down from the wall to his son Hector, who stood still before the gate, unshakably resolved to fight with Achilles. Stretching out his hands to him, the old man spoke in a pitiful voice. "Hector," he said, "dear child, I beg and beseech you not to stand and fight with that man. He is stronger than you by far, and he has a heart of steel. Many of my sons he has killed already, and even today I miss the sight of two others, Lycaon and Polydorus. Bitterly I grieve for them, if indeed they are dead; but how much greater would be my grief and the grief of all the Trojans, if you were to fall before Achilles! Come inside the walls, I beg you, and save us as you always have done. Have pity on me, your father, and think of the fate that is coming upon me in my old age—to see my wife and daughters dragged away by the Greeks, my sons all butchered and my palaces burnt with fire. And I myself shall lie dead among the ruins of my kingdom, and the dogs that I have fed at my own table will lick up my blood. When a young man is killed in battle and lies dead, he still looks beautiful with his wounds upon him. But there is nothing more pitiful than the sight of an old man with his flesh hacked to pieces and his grey hair and beard all foul with slaughter."

So Priam spoke in agony of mind, and Hecuba too, his wife, cried out to her son Hector from the wall. She drew her dress aside, showing him her breast, and she said to him: "Hector, my child, have pity on me! Think of how often I have given you milk from this breast and have put you to sleep. Do not fight with this man alone, my darling child. He is pitiless and, if he kills you, neither I nor your wife will be able to weep over your body and to bury you. Far away from us two the dogs will devour you by the Greek ships."

So Hector's father and mother wept as they begged him not to risk his dear life; but Hector stood firm, resting his bright shield on a protruding part of the wall, watching great Achilles draw near. "If now," he was thinking to himself, "I were to withdraw to safety, Polydamas would reproach me for not taking his advice this day and for not avoiding this disastrous battle. 'Hector trusted in his own strength,' people will be saying, 'and lost the army.' It would have been better far if I had taken his advice; but now at least I can preserve my own honour and either kill Achilles or be killed by him fighting in front of my city."

And now Achilles was upon him, looking like the God of War himself, shaking in his hand his terrible ashen spear, brilliant in his armour like the rising sun. As Hector looked at him, his heart failed him and he turned to escape. But Achilles darted after him like a falcon, which is the swiftest thing on wings, chasing a dove and darting after her as she twists and turns in her efforts to escape. So Hector fled before Achilles, running beneath the walls of Troy. They swept past the fig-tree and past the two springs of Scamander with the beautiful troughs of stone where the wives and daughters of the Trojans used to wash their shining clothes in the days of peace, before the coming of the Greeks. Past these fair springs they ran, and they ran like champions. But this was no ordinary foot race with an ox or a shield for prize; here the prize for which they struggled was nothing less than the life of horsetaming Hector.

Three times on their swift feet they circled the city of Priam, and from Olympus all the gods were watching them as they ran. At last Zeus spoke to the other gods and said: "Alas! the man whom I see being pursued around the walls is one who is very dear to me. My heart is sad for Hector, who has so often burned sacrifices to me on the peaks of Ida and in the high citadel of Troy. He is a good man and I wish that I could save him from the hands of Achilles."

The bright-eyed goddess Athene answered him. "Father," she said, "how can you say such things? The man is mortal and the day of his fate has come. How then could you wish to preserve him?"

"It is true," Zeus replied to her. "Do with him as you wish," and Athene who already had been longing for her father's permission, darted down from Olympus to the Trojan plain.

Still the two men ran with Achilles always heading Hector off from the town and towards the plain. It was like running in a dream, when the pursuer can never quite catch up with the pursued and the pursued can never quite escape from his pursuer, and both seem, though they are putting out every effort, hardly to be moving at all.

Now however Zeus took his golden scales. In one of the balances he put the life of Achilles and in the other the life of Hector. He held the scales by the middle and Hector's life sank downwards towards Hades. Apollo, who had strengthened his feet, now left him, but Athene came to the side of Achilles and said to him: "Now, Achilles, the time for our triumph has come. Even Apollo cannot preserve Hector now. Wait here and recover your breath and I will go to Hector and persuade him to fight with you."

Achilles was glad when he heard her words. He stopped in his course and stood still, leaning on his heavy spear.

Athene then went to Hector and, putting on the shape and the voice of his brother Deiphobus, she stood at his side and said: "Brother, you are weary with running from great Achilles. Now let me stand by you and let us fight him together."

"Deiphobus," Hector replied, "I always loved you the best of all my brothers, and now I love you still more, since you are the only one who has dared to come outside the wall and stand at my side. Now let us see whether Achilles will kill the two of us or whether perhaps he may fall first to my spear."

So he and Achilles came near to each other. Great Hector was the first to speak. "Achilles," he said, "I shall run from you no longer. Now let us fight face to face and either kill or be killed. But let us first make a promise and call the gods to witness it. If Zeus gives me the victory, I will do nothing outrageous to your body, but will give it back to your friends for burial, once I have stripped it of its armour. Will you promise to do the same for me?"

Achilles glared at him and replied: "Hector, there can be no promises and agreements between men and lions or between wolves and sheep. So it is between you and me. There is nothing but undying hatred. Now is the time for you to show all the courage you have and all your skill with the spear; for now in a moment you will pay me back for all the pain I felt for my comrades whom you have destroyed."

As he spoke he raised his great spear and hurled it. But Hector was watching him closely; he sank down on one knee and the spear flew over his shoulder and stuck in the ground. He did not see, however, that Athene took it up and put it back again into Achilles' hands.

Now Hector prepared to throw his spear, but first he cried out: "You missed me, Achilles. It seems that you were over-confident. Now avoid this spear of mine if you can. I only pray that it may be buried in your flesh."

Then he hurled his long-shadowed spear and struck the shield of Achilles full in the centre. But the god's handi-work was not so easily pierced and the spear point was blunted on the massy metal. Hector was angry that the weapon had left his hand and done no harm to his enemy. He saw that Achilles still grasped a spear while he himself had no other to throw, and he shouted to Deiphobus, telling him to hand him a spear quickly. But when he looked round, Deiphobus was nowhere to be seen. Then Hector knew what had happened. "Alas!" he said. "Now it is certain that the gods are calling me to my death. I thought that strong Deiphobus was here with me, but he is inside the walls and I have been cheated by Athene. Now sad death is very close to me and can no longer be escaped. So it has seemed good to Zeus and to Apollo who used to love me and protect me. My fate is upon me, but at least I shall go to meet it and die bravely, so that those who are still unborn will hear how Hector died."

Then he drew his sharp and heavy sword and whirling it above his head, he swooped upon Achilles like an eagle that, from the height of the sky, swoops through the black clouds to snatch up from the earth a lamb or a cowering hare. Achilles rushed to meet him and his heart was filled with savage anger. He held his great shield before him and above the shield nodded the crest of the beautiful helmet that Hephaestus had made for him. In his right hand he poised his spear, and its glittering point shone bright as the Evening Star which shines through the darkness with the other stars and is the brightest and most beautiful of them all. So he came on with burning anger in his eyes and he searched the strong body of Hector for the spot where the flesh would most easily yield to his spear.

He saw that most of the body was covered with the flashing armour that he had taken from the dead Patroclus, but there was a place on the neck by the collar-bone, a place where death comes most quickly, which was unprotected. It was at this place that Achilles aimed as Hector charged upon him and with a powerful thrust he drove the heavy spear clean through the neck, cleaving the tender flesh but not severing the wind-pipe so that it was still possible for Hector to speak.

Hector fell in the dust and Achilles stood in triumph over him. "Hector," he said, "when you stripped the armour from Patroclus, you thought you would live to wear it. You did not remember that by the hollow ships there was a champion waiting, a mightier man than Patroclus, yes, I myself who have loosed your knees in battle. And now your body will be torn to pieces by the dogs and the vultures while the Greeks bury Patroclus with honour."

There was little life left in Hector and he spoke with labouring breath. "I beg you," he said, "by your own life and the life of your parents, do not let the dogs devour me by the ships. Take the gold that Priam will offer you in ransom and give him back my body so that the Trojans and their wives may give it burial."

Achilles looked at him grimly. "You dog," he said, "do not mention my parents to me or my life. I wish I had the heart to cut your body to pieces and to eat it raw, so much I hate you. Be sure of this. I shall accept no ransom, not if it were twenty times your worth in gold. Nor will anything keep the dogs and the birds from eating every fragment of your flesh."

Hector, now at the point of dying, spoke once more. "Indeed I know you for what you are. The heart in your breast is hard as iron, and I would never have persuaded you. Yet think what you are doing, lest the gods are angry with you on the day when you too, for all your strength, will lie by the Scaean Gate, killed by Paris and by Apollo."

As he spoke, death closed his eyes; his soul sped out of his limbs and went down to Hades, lamenting its fate, leaving behind its manhood and its youth.

Achilles spoke to the dead body. "Die!" he said, "As for me, let my death come when Zeus and the other immortal gods send it to me."

Then he drew his spear out of the wound and stripped the bloodstained armour from the body. And now the other Greeks came to see the sight. They stared in wonder at the size of Hector and at his beauty. Many of them stabbed him with their spears. "Look," they would say to each other, "it is much safer to come near Hector now than at the time when he was burning our ships."

But Achilles turned to the leaders of the Greeks and said: "Friends, we have won a great victory and the gods have granted us the power to kill this man who did us more harm than all the rest put together. Now there still lies unburied by my ships the body of my friend, Patroclus whom I can never forget so long as I live, and even in Hades, though the dead forget their dear ones, I shall still remember my comrade. Now let us go and bury him and as we go let us sing in triumph, for we have killed Hector, whom the Trojans worshipped as though he were a god."

Then Achilles did a terrible thing. He cut through the tendons of Hector's feet from heel to ankle, bound them with leather thongs which he threaded through, and fastened the thongs to his chariot. Then he mounted his chariot and drove back over the plain dragging the body of Hector behind him, with the dark hair streaming backward, and the face that was once so beautiful jolted on the stony ground and in the deep dust. So Zeus allowed the body of Hector to be ill-treated by his enemies, there, on his own native ground.

Meanwhile old Priam and Hecuba and the Trojans had been watching from the walls. Now when they saw the head of Hector draggled in the dust they raised a loud and terrible cry as though the whole of towering Troy were going up in flames. King Priam struggled toward the gates, and his friends with difficulty held him back. "Ah, friends!" he said, "let me go. Let me go alone to plead with this savage man. He may have reverence for my age and for my grey hair. He also has a father who is old as I am and who loves him. Ah! how many of my sons has he killed in this fearful war? Yet for all of them I do not grieve as I do for this one, for Hector. How I wish that he had died in my arms! Then his mother and I could have satisfied our hearts with weeping for him."

So Priam spoke and the Trojans wept as they listened to him. Then Hecuba cried out to the women who were about her: "My child, how can I go on living now that you are dead? Day and night you were my joy and comfort. You were our great defence and the Trojans looked up to you as to a god. But now Fate and Death have overtaken you."

So Hecuba wept and lamented and the women joined her in the lament. But Hector's wife had not yet heard what had happened to her husband, or that he had remained alone outside the walls. She was sitting in her lofty house and weaving at the loom. She had just called to her servants and told them to put a great cauldron on the fire so that there should be hot water for Hector's bath when he came back from the battle. Little did she know that he was far indeed from the refreshment of baths and of changed clothing, lying dead upon the plain, destroyed by Athene and by Achilles.

Now she heard the noise of the crying and wailing from the walls. Her limbs trembled and the shuttle dropped from her hand. Once more she called to her servants. "Come with me, two of you," she said, "and help to support me. I must go and see what has happened. That was the voice of my husband's mother that I heard, and now my heart is in my mouth and my legs will hardly carry me. I pray that what I think may not be true, but I am terribly afraid that Achilles may have caught my husband alone outside the walls. For Hector would never stay with the crowd; he always went out far in front of the rest and would let no one be as brave as he was."

Then she ran from the house as though she was mad and her servants followed her. She came to the tower above the gate, and, looking out over the plain, she saw her husband being dragged in the dust behind the swift horses of Achilles towards the Greek camp. Then the blackness of night fell upon her eyes; fainting, she fell backwards and her shining head-dress dropped to the ground, her bright coronet and the veil that golden Aphrodite had given her on the day that great Hector had come to her father's house to make her his bride.

As she lay there the noble women of Troy came to her and supported her head, and when she was able to speak she spoke to them between her sobs and said: "O Hector, Hector, I am unhappy. One evil fate has destroyed us both. Now you are going to the house of Hades and I am left a widow in your house. And the child whom we had together is still only a little boy. You will not be able to help him, Hector, since you are dead, nor will he be able to help you. Even if he escapes from this terrible war, there will be nothing in his life but sorrow and trouble. For when a child loses his father he loses his friends too. The other boys, whose fathers are still living, will push him away from their feasts. And he will come running to me in tears, Astyanax, who always used to sit on his father's knee and eat nothing but the best pieces of meat, and when he was sleepy and tired of play always slept in a soft bed in his nurse's arms and never wanted for anything. But now that he has lost his dear father, his whole life will be miserable, Astyanax, 'lord of the City,' so the Trojans call him, since it was you, Hector, who were the one protection to us all. And now, far from your parents, you lie by the Greek ships and the wriggling worms will eat your body after the dogs and the vultures have sated themselves. Naked you lie there, in spite of the fine clothing that I have here for you in your house. All this clothing I shall burn in the fire, since you will never wear it again."

So she spoke weeping and all the women lamented with her.

XVIII

THE FUNERAL AND THE GAMES

MEANWHILE ACHILLES, dragging the body of Hector behind his chariot, had led his troops back to their camp. Before they unyoked the horses they drove their chariots three times past the body of Patroclus to do him honour, and wept as they drove past him, so that all the sandy ground was wet with their tears. Then Achilles laid his man-killing hands on the breast of his comrade and cried out: "Rejoice, Patroclus, even though you are in the House of the Dead. I have done for you what I promised to do. I have dragged Hector here and shall give his body to the dogs to tear in pieces; and at your funeral I shall cut the throats of twelve young nobles of Troy to satisfy my anger."

Then he loosed the body of Hector from his chariot and let it lie face-downwards in the dust by the bier of Patroclus. The Myrmidons unyoked their horses and sat down to a great funeral feast. There were white oxen, sheep and goats to be eaten, and great fat hogs with their gleaming tusks. Cupfuls of blood were poured around the dead body.

But Achilles himself with the other kings went to feast with Agamemnon. When he arrived at the hut, Agamemnon told his servants to put a great cauldron on the fire, so that Achilles might wash the blood from his body and refresh himself. But Achilles refused. "I swear by Zeus," he said, "that no water shall come near my body until I have buried Patroclus. For I shall never, so long as I am alive, feel such pain as I feel now. I must eat, I know, though still all food is distasteful to me. And tomorrow, if King Agamemnon agrees, let men go out early and fetch wood for the funeral pyre."

Agamemnon willingly agreed. They sat down to their dinner and, when their hunger and thirst were satisfied, they went back each to his own camp. But Achilles lay down by the shore of the breaking sea in an open place where the waves came surging up on to the beach. Here he lay down and he groaned deeply as he lay there; but soon sleep came and enfolded him, making him forget his cares and his weariness, for his strong limbs were tired out by the fighting and by the chase of Hector round the walls of windy Troy.

Now in his sleep the ghost of Patroclus came to him, looking just like he had been when he was alive, with the same eyes and expression of the face, with the same voice and wearing the same clothes. The ghost stood by Achilles' head and spoke to him. "You are asleep, Achilles, and have forgotten about me, though when I was alive you used never to forget me. Bury me at once, so that I may pass through the gates of the House of the Dead. For now the other souls keep me out and will not let me pass the River. And give me your hand, I beg you. Once I have been burned in the flames I shall never come back again from Hades; nor will you and I ever sit apart by ourselves and talk as we used to do. Dreadful Fate has overwhelmed me, and it is your fate too, great Achilles, to die beneath the walls of Troy. One other thing I ask from you. Just as we grew up together in our youth, so let our bones rest side by side and our ashes be mingled in the same urn."

"Patroclus, dear friend," said Achilles, "why have you come to tell me this? Be sure that I shall do everything as you would have it done. But come nearer to me, so that we may embrace each other for a short moment and find comfort in each other's grief."

As he spoke he stretched out his arms to clasp his dead friend, but the ghost slipped away from him like smoke and with a thin cry disappeared beneath the earth. Achilles woke in amazement and cried out: "It is true then that even in the House of the Dead there is something of us that remains, though it is only a ghost and an image without life or sense. For all through the night the ghost of poor Patroclus has been standing by my head, weeping and lamenting, telling me what it wanted done. It looked just like Patroclus himself."

By crying out Achilles had woken the Myrmidons, and now he and they mourned once more for Patroclus until dawn. But at dawn King Agamemnon sent out men and mules to fetch wood from Mount Ida. There they felled the tall oaks, cut the timber into lengths and brought it back to the place appointed by Achilles for the funeral pyre. To this place had come the Myrmidons with their horses and their chariots, escorting the body of Patroclus. From the wood that had been brought they raised a great pyre, a hundred feet high and a hundred feet broad. Sad at heart, they placed the body on the top, and all around the body they placed the carcases of sheep and oxen. There were four great war horses also that Achilles sacrificed at the pyre and there too he put jars of honey and of oil. Patroclus had had nine dogs as pets. Achilles cut the throats of two of these and put them also on the pyre. Then he did a terrible thing: he killed twelve Trojan prisoners, good and noble men, and put their bodies on to the flames so that they should burn with Patroclus. The wind fanned the flames into a great fire and Achilles cried out for the last time to his friend. "Farewell, Patroclus!" he said. "I have kept the promises that I made. I have killed twelve noble Trojans who will burn with you in the fire. As for Hector, I shall not give his body to the flames but leave it for the dogs to tear apart."

Yet for all this the dogs never came near the body of Hector. Day and night Aphrodite, daughter of Zeus, kept them away from him and over his flesh she poured an ambrosial oil of roses so that it should not be torn when Achilles dragged him over the ground. And Apollo folded the body in a purple cloud that covered the space where it lay and warded off the fierce rays of the sun, so that the skin should not be withered or corrupted.

Through the afternoon and through the night the fire burned, and at daybreak, as the flames sank down, they poured wine upon the ashes and carefully collected together the bones of Patroclus. At the orders of Achilles they put the bones in a golden urn and sealed it. "Let them lie there," he said, "until the time when I too have gone down to the House of the Dead. And let us build a mound for him that is fitting but not very big. Later those of you who are still alive can build a bigger tomb where my bones can be buried together with his."

Quickly the soldiers of the Greeks built the tomb for Patroclus and then Achilles brought out from his ships valuable and splendid prizes and prepared to hold funeral games in honour of his friend. The troops sat down in a great circle and watched while the greatest and most skilful athletes in the army competed in the games.

The first event was the chariot race, and the first prize was a slave woman well trained in household matters and a great tripod, very exquisitely made. The second prize was a mare known to be good for breeding, the third prize a new copper vessel that had never been touched by the flames. And for those who came fourth and fifth there were prizes of two talents of gold and another cooking vessel.

The first to come forward for the race was Eumelus, who had some of the best horses in the army and was himself a famous charioteer. Others who competed were Diomedes, who drove the fine horses that he had taken from Aeneas, Menelaus, Meriones and Nestor's son, Antilochus. Before the race began Nestor gave long and careful advice to Antilochus. He told him that he would never win on the merits of his horses, since they were the slowest ones in the race, but that skill and judgment in racing are often just as valuable as speed.

Soon the horses were off and the drivers were shouting to the horses as they sped over the plain in a cloud of dust, vanishing from the eyes of the spectators. At the turning post Eumelus was ahead, but Diomedes was quickly over-hauling him. Apollo, however, was angry with Diomedes and, just as he was going to overtake Eumelus, the god knocked the whip out of his hand. In despair Diomedes saw Eumelus's horses going ahead while his own began to slacken pace. But Athene was watching over her favourite. She brought back his whip to him and set it in his hand. Then she went after Eumelus and broke the yoke of his chariot, so that the horses ran on wildly and Eumelus himself was hurled to the ground. As he got to his feet, bruised and sore from his fall, he saw the chariot of Diomedes sweep past him, now certain to win the first prize.

Menelaus was not far behind, and behind Menelaus came Antilochus. Not far from the winning post the chariot track ran through a narrow gorge and at this point Antilochus whipped up his horses and, driving a little to the side of the main track, overtook Menelaus and began to come closer and closer to him so that he would force him off the course. Menelaus shouted out to him: "Antilochus, this is mad driving, wait till the track gets wider and then pass me if you can. Otherwise both our chariots will be wrecked."

But Antilochus pretended not to hear, and drove even faster. Finally, fearing that they would both be killed, Menelaus gave way and Antilochus drove past him. Again Menelaus shouted out: "You are the most dangerous driver I have ever seen—absolutely without sense, and I shall complain about this foul." Then he lashed on his own horses and, as soon as the track became wider, they began to gain upon Antilochus and would have passed him if the course had been longer As it was, however, Antilochus just managed to come in second, with Menelaus close behind him. Meriones came fourth, and last of all came Eumelus, dragging his broken chariot.

Achilles was sorry for him and said: "Eumelus is the best driver of them all and he has come in last, through no fault of his own. He ought to have a prize. Let us give him the second prize, since Diomedes certainly should have the first."

Everyone agreed to this except Antilochus who said: "Great Achilles, I came in second and I ought not to lose my prize. If you feel so sorry for Eumelus, you ought to give him something else."

Achilles liked Antilochus and he smiled at this. "Very well," he said, "you shall keep the mare and I will give Eumelus a splendid Trojan breastplate. Then everyone will be satisfied."

But now Menelaus, in great anger, came forward to swear that it was only by a foul that Antilochus had managed to beat him and he challenged Antilochus to swear an oath to the contrary. At this Antilochus began to be ashamed. "Forgive me, King Menelaus," he said. "You are older than I am and you know how young men sometimes go too far in the heat of the moment. I do not want to quarrel with you and I will give you the mare and also something else of my own, if it will please you and make you forget your anger."

Menelaus at once forgave him. "Antilochus," he said, "you have fought well in my cause and I respect both your father and yourself. And I know that usually you do not act so foolishly as you did today. So I will give you back the mare and will cease to be angry with you."

So Menelaus took the third prize and Meriones the fourth. There was no one to claim the fifth prize and Achilles gave it to Nestor, saying to him: "My Lord, accept this, I beg you, in memory of Patroclus. I think that you are too old now to compete yourself in the wrestling or the foot races, and I should like you to have something by which to remember my dead friend."

Old Nestor thanked him. "You are quite right," he said. "There was a time when I could run and box and wrestle with any man in Greece. But I am not so quick on my feet as I was, nor so strong in the arm. Now I thank you for your gift and for showing me the respect which you never forget to show. I pray that the gods will reward you."

And now came the other events. There was boxing, throwing the javelin and throwing the discus. In the wrestling match the competitors were great Ajax and Odysseus. For long the two remained gripped together and neither was able to move the other. The sweat streamed from their bodies as each exerted his enormous strength, and along their arms and on their ribs the flesh reddened beneath the pressure of their holds. Finally Ajax said to Odysseus: "My Lord Odysseus, we must allow each other a throw each and then see to whom Zeus will give the victory." So he lifted Odysseus off the ground, but Odysseus knew every trick in wrestling. As he was raised in the air he kicked Ajax behind the knee and brought him down on his back, himself springing on to his chest. There was loud applause at this. And now in the next round Odysseus tried to lift Ajax and throw him. He could hardly shift the great bulk, and though, by crooking his knee behind, he tried to force Ajax backwards, they both fell to the ground together. They then prepared for a third round, but Achilles prevented them. "You have both won," he said, "and the prizes shall be equal." After their struggle Ajax and Odysseus were glad enough to agree.

Next came the foot race. Among the runners was another Ajax called Ajax the Smaller, since he was not such a giant of a man as was the Ajax who had just wrestled; but he was a great warrior and one of the finest runners among the Greeks. The other competitors were the wise Odysseus and Antilochus, who was the best runner among the younger men. The first prize for this event was a beautiful mixing bowl of silver; the second prize was a fine large ox, and the third was a talent of gold.

This race was a very close one. Ajax kept just a little ahead of Odysseus, but Odysseus was so near to him that Ajax could feel his breath upon his shoulder. All the army cheered Odysseus for the effort he was making and, as they approached the winning post, Odysseus prayed to Athene, begging her to strengthen his limbs. Athene heard his prayer. She made his limbs lighter and at the same time she caused Ajax to slip and fall in a place that was all slippery from the dung of cattle that had been standing there for the sacrifices at the tomb of Patroclus. So Odysseus won the first prize. Ajax took the ox and, as he held it by its horns, he spat out of his mouth the filth into which he had fallen. When he recovered his breath, he gasped out: "Sure enough it was the goddess who made me lose, Athene who always looks after Odysseus as though she were his mother."

The others laughed at him. As for Antilochus, he took the third prize and, as he took it, he said: "Friends, it is always the same thing. It is the old ones whom the gods love. For though Ajax is only a little older than I am, Odysseus belongs to an earlier generation altogether. Yet he is tough enough. None of us could beat him in a race, except Achilles."

Achilles was pleased with the praise. "Antilochus," he said, "I thank you for the compliment and in return I will double your prize and make it two talents of gold."

So Antilochus took the two talents and was highly pleased with his prize.

The prize for the next event was the armour of Sarpedon, whom Patroclus had killed. Two men were to fight for this armour in single combat and the winner should be the one who first drew blood. Great Ajax and Diomedes were the two competitors here. Three times they charged at each other with their spears and at the fourth charge Ajax drove his spear right through Diomedes' shield; but the bronze breastplate warded off the point from his body. Then Diomedes lunged over the top of Ajax's shield and just managed to touch him on the neck. The army cried out in terror, fearing lest one or other of these two great champions should receive a serious wound, and Achilles stopped the fight and decided that the armour should be shared between the two.

Next came a contest in archery. Here the prizes were iron axes. There was a set of ten double-headed axes for the winner and a set of ten single-headed axes for the loser. The greatest archer in the army was Teucer, the brother of Ajax, but Meriones, the friend of Idomeneus, was not far his inferior. These were the two who now competed for the axes. Nor was the competition an easy one. A pigeon was tied by the foot to the top of one of a ship's masts a long way away from the arena. This was the target, and to choose the one who should shoot first, two pebbles were shaken together in a bronze helmet. Teucer's pebble was the first to jump out of the helmet, and he immediately put an arrow to his bow and shot. But he had forgotten first to pray to Apollo, the god of Archery, and so he missed the pigeon, though his arrow struck the cord by which it was tied and cut through it. The Greeks all cheered, since the shot was certainly a good one; but Meriones quickly snatched the bow from Teucer's hand and, as the pigeon, now free from its cord, shot up into the sky, he hastily made his prayer to Apollo and shot at the bird at the moment when it was high in the air above his head. The arrow went clean through the bird's wing and came down again to stick in the earth at Meriones' feet. The pigeon fluttered weakly down to settle on a ship's mast and from there fell dead to the ground. Everyone was amazed at such shooting and Meriones took the set of double axes.

And now the games were over. The Greeks went back to their tents to prepare for their evening meal and for their sleep.

XIX

THE END OF THE ANGER

BUT ACHILLES could not forget his dead comrade. At night he tossed to and fro on his bed, longing for the good and strong man who had been his friend, thinking of all the joys and sorrows that they had been through together, all the battles and expeditions on land and all the perils on the waves of the sea.

He would rise before dawn from his sleepless bed and would wander along the beach and promontories of the land. And when dawn came he would yoke his horses to his chariot, tie the body of Hector behind the chariot wheels, and then drag him three times round the tomb of Patroclus. Afterwards he would go back to his hut, leaving the body on its face stretched out in the dust. But Apollo still loved Hector, though he was dead, and kept the body fair and beautiful, guarding it from all corruption and from all the injuries that Achilles did to it in his rage.

Zeus himself was angry with Achilles for so shamefully treating his fallen enemy, and so were the other blessed gods and goddesses except for Hera and Athene who still hated the Trojans and the whole house of Priam. But Zeus would not be governed by his wife and by his daughter. He sent for the goddess Thetis and she came to him from the deep sea cave where she had been sitting with her sister nymphs. Then the Father of Gods and Men spoke to her and said: "I have done for you what you asked. Achilles has won great glory and is honoured by the Greeks more than ever before. Now I wish you to go to him and tell him that I am displeased with him for keeping the body of Hector, who was a good man and one whom I loved. Let him give it back. Meanwhile I shall send my messenger Iris to old Priam and tell him to prepare a ransom and to go and plead with Achilles."

Thetis, the silver-footed goddess, was not slow to obey. She darted down from the heights of Olympus and came to Achilles whom she found still mourning by his hut. "Dear child," she said to him, as she took his hand in hers, "will you not take any pleasure in life? Can you not eat and drink or find comfort in a woman's love? Your own fate is close upon you and it is only a little time that you have left to live." Then she gave him the message from Father Zeus and Achilles replied: "Let it be so. If Zeus commands me, I must obey. When they bring the ransom, they shall have the body."

Meanwhile Zeus had sent his messenger Iris, the goddess of the rainbow, to Priam in Troy. In the royal palace she found nothing but wailing and lamentation. Priam was sitting with his sons around him. The old man had be-fouled his head with dust and he covered his face with his cloak as the tears still streamed from his eyes. And all through the house his daughters and his sons' wives were crying out and weeping as they remembered Hector and all the other brave men who had fallen before Achilles and the Greeks.

Iris went up to the old man and spoke gently in his ear; but his limbs began to tremble when he heard her voice. "Do not be afraid, Priam," she said. "I have not come to you with news of evil, but have come to help you. I am the messenger of Zeus who, though he is far away, still cares for you and pities you. It is the will of Zeus that you should go to Achilles with a ransom for your son. You must go alone, but you need have no fear. Hermes himself will protect you and Achilles will do you no harm."

After speaking these words Iris vanished from sight. Priam at once told his sons to get ready for him a cart with mules to draw it. Then he went to his high-roofed bedroom with its panels and roof of cedar wood, and he called to his wife Hecuba and told her of the message which had come to him from Zeus. But Hecuba cried out in despair when she heard that he intended to go to the Greek ships. "Dear husband," she said, "have you taken leave of your wits, you whom everyone used to admire for your wisdom? How can you bear to go and put yourself into the power of that cruel and savage man who has killed so many of our sons? Certainly he will kill you too."

But Priam refused to be turned aside from his purpose. "Do not try to hold me back," he said. "I tell you that I saw the goddess with my own eyes, and I am going to do as she told me. Even if it is my fate to die by the Greek ships, it is a fate that I would accept. Once I have held my son in my arms and wept over him, then I do not mind if Achilles strikes me down with his murderous hands."

Out of the treasure chambers of his palace Priam then took twelve beautiful robes, with tunics and cloaks. He took ten talents of gold, two burnished tripods, four cauldrons and a drinking cup of very great beauty which had once been given to him by the Thracians when he had made a journey into their country.

So impatient was he to be on his way that he shouted angrily at his sons, at Paris and Helenus and Deiphobus and the rest, since they seemed to him to be slow in harnessing the mules to the cart. "All my best sons," he cried, "are dead and gone. You who are left are good for nothing but dancing and wearing fine clothes. I wish that all of you had died and left Hector alive, who was like a god among men and looked not like a man's son but like the son of a god. Make the cart ready immediately and load it with these treasures, so that I can be on my way."

Priam's sons trembled at the old man's angry voice. They hurriedly brought out the cart and harnessed the mules to it. Then they fetched the gifts which Priam had chosen for the ransom and loaded them carefully upon the cart. The old king mounted and took the reins. As he drove through the streets of Troy a crowd followed him, weeping and wailing as if he were going to his death. His sons and his old counsellors escorted him outside the city gates. Then they turned back and Priam went on alone.

As he crossed the plain towards the ships of the Greeks, darkness began to descend and suddenly through the darkness Priam saw approaching him a young man of great beauty. He stopped still in terror, fearing that this must be one of the princes or captains of the Greeks who would betray him. But the young man was no other than the god Hermes, guide to travellers and bringer of good fortune, whom Zeus had sent down from Olympus to protect King Priam. Hermes soon calmed the old man's fears and promised to accompany him to the hut of Achilles. Not yet did Priam realise that he had a divine escort; but when they reached the Greek camp, they found that all the sentries were asleep, since the god had exercised his power over them; and when they reached that part of the camp where Achilles had his quarters, they found the entrance barred by a great bolt made from the trunk of a pine tree, which could only be moved by the strength of three men. Hermes by himself easily drew back this bolt. Then he turned to Priam and said to him: "I, who have accompanied you here, am an immortal god. My father Zeus sent me to help you. But now I shall go no further with you. Go in yourself and pray to Achilles in the name of his father and of his mother and of his own son to have pity on your distress."

Hermes then returned to Olympus. Priam went forward to the hut and opened the door. Inside he saw Achilles with some of his companions about him. Automedon, the charioteer, was waiting on him and Achilles had just finished eating and drinking. Great Priam entered, and no one saw him until he was standing close to Achilles and until he had knelt on the ground and was clasping his knees and kissing his hands, those terrible murderous hands that had destroyed Hector and so many of the old man's sons. As they saw him they were filled with astonishment, and they listened still in amazement while Priam spoke. "Royal Achilles," he said, "think of your own father who is an old man too, like I am. Perhaps he is being attacked by his neighbours and has no one near him to help and protect him; yet, even so, while he knows that you are alive, he will be glad at heart and every day he will hope to see his dear son again, coming back from Troy. But I have nothing to look forward to. I had nineteen sons, the best sons of any man in Troy. Most of them have fallen in battle and Hector, who was everything to me, who was the one great defence of Troy and the Trojans, has been killed by you fighting for his country. Now I have come with a splendid ransom for his body. Give him back to me, I beg you. Have reverence for the gods, Achilles, and have pity upon me, remembering your own father. Indeed I am still more to be pitied than he is, since I have forced myself to do something which no one else on earth has done: I have kissed the hands which killed my own son."

As he spoke, Achilles began to think with pain and longing of his own father. He took the old man's hand and gently moved him from his knees. Then both he and Priam burst into tears, Priam on the ground at Achilles' feet weeping for Hector, and Achilles weeping for his own father and for Patroclus. And when for the time he had had his fill of weeping, Achilles rose from his chair and took the old man by the hand to raise him to his feet, pitying and reverencing his grey hair and beard. "Indeed," he said, "I pity you. How you have suffered in your heart! You have dared to come alone to the Greek ships and to me who have killed so many of your fine sons. Now sit down, I beg you, and in spite of our grief, let us cease our lamentations, since they cannot bring back what is past. It is the will of the gods, who live in happiness for ever, that we wretched mortals should be in pain either constantly or from time to time. None of us can escape it. Consider my father Peleus. From his birth the gods gave him all their most splendid gifts. He had wealth and fortune beyond all other men; he was King of the Myrmidons; and, though he was a mortal, he had a goddess for his wife. Yet to him too the gods gave evil as well as good. He has no children to carry on his name, none except for me who am doomed to die young. Nor do I help to care for him in his old age, since I stay here, far from my own country, bringing harm to you and to your children. You too, sir, had the name of being happy with one of the greatest kingdoms in the world and with so many noble and brave sons. Yet ever since the gods brought this war upon you, you have seen nothing but battles and the killing of men. You must endure therefore and find courage to bear your fate. No weeping will ever bring your son back to life again."

Priam replied to him and said: "Do not ask me to sit down, Prince Achilles, while Hector still lies uncared for. Accept the ransom and let me see him with my eyes. And I pray that you yourself may return to your own land in safety, since you have spared my life."

Achilles looked sternly at the old man. "Do not hurry me or reproach me," he said, "lest my anger should return and I should sin against Zeus by treating you as I treated Hector. I have already resolved to give him back to you. Indeed I know that it was by the help of some god that you came here, for otherwise you could never have passed the sentries or drawn back the bolt at my gate. Do as I say, therefore, and do not anger me."

Priam trembled at his words and seated himself on a chair. Achilles then rushed out of doors like a lion. He gave orders for the ransom to be taken from the cart and for the body of

Hector to be washed and anointed with oil and wrapped in fine coverlets. Then he lifted the body in his own arms and set it on a bier which his comrades raised up and put upon the waggon. When this was done he groaned aloud and spoke the name of his dear friend. "Patroclus," he said, "do not be angry with me if in the House of Death you learn that I have given back the body of Hector to his father. He has given me a noble ransom, and you too shall have your share of it."

Then Achilles returned to his hut and sat down opposite Priam. "Sir," he said, "I have done as you asked. Your son's body is lying on a bier and at dawn you shall see him and shall take him away. Tomorrow you shall weep for him when you bring him back into Troy. And indeed you have reason to weep."

After this food and drink were set before them, and when their hunger was satisfied, Priam looked long and carefully at Achilles and wondered at his size and beauty; for he looked like an immortal god. Achilles also gazed with admiration at Priam, noting his great stature, his noble looks, and listening to the words he spoke. Thus they found pleasure in looking at each other, but presently King Priam said: "Achilles, I would ask you now to let me retire to rest. Sweet sleep has never yet come to my eyes since the time that Hector lost his life at your hands, nor until now have I tasted food and drink."

Achilles rose and had a bed made for the old man in a covered place outside his own room. But before Priam retired to rest he asked him how many days they would require in Troy to hold the funeral of Hector. "I will promise you," he said, "that you will be left free to bury him as you think fit. There will be no fighting till the funeral is over."

Priam thanked Achilles and told him that the Trojans would mourn for Hector in their houses for nine days, on the tenth day they would bury him and on the eleventh build his tomb. "And on the twelfth," he said, "we will fight, if fight we must."

Then Achilles grasped the old man's hand to assure him that his promise would be kept and to free him from fear. He escorted him to the bed that had been prepared for him and himself lay down to sleep upon his own bed.

But before dawn Hermes, whom Zeus had appointed to protect Priam, came to the old man's bed and woke him. He wished him to pass through the Greek lines before the army was awake, and Priam obeyed the orders of the god. Hermes himself yoked the mules; he drew back the heavy bolt from the gate and he drove the waggon, with Hector's body upon it, as far as the ford in the eddying stream of Scamander. Now dawn was showing red in the eastern sky, and Hermes departed to Olympus, while Priam drove the horses on towards the city, carrying their sad burden.

King Priam's daughter Cassandra was the first to see him coming over the plain. She had climbed to the top of the wall and now she let her voice ring out over Troy. "Men and women of Troy," she said, "you who used to rejoice when Hector, our deliverer, came back from battle, come out and see him now."

Then every man and woman in the city came out into the streets, and when they saw the body of Hector, they were overcome by unspeakable grief, crowding round the waggon where the corpse lay. But Priam told his people to make way for him so that he could take the body to its own home. There would be time later, he said, for them to mourn for Hector, but first he must be mourned for by his own family.

So they brought the body into the palace and laid it down on a bed, and summoned the musicians to make their music, and to sing the dirges. And among the women Andromache, holding Hector's head between her hands, began the lament. "Husband," she said, "you died young, before your time, and you have left me behind you a widow with our little boy who will never grow up, I think, to be a man. Before then this city with all its towers will be folded up in flames, since you, Hector, its guardian and defender, have died. And I shall be carried away into slavery, and you, my little son, will go with me, unless one of the Greeks seizes you by the arm and hurls you down from the battlements to your death, angry with you because Hector killed a brother of his or a father or a son. For there were many Greeks who fell before the spear of Hector, and in the hard fighting your father had no gentle ways. That is why all the people lament for him. But, Hector, my sorrow is greatest of all, because you did not die in bed, holding out your arms to me, nor did you speak to me your last words, so that I could have treasured them in my heart day and night as I wept for you."

So she spoke and all the women wept with her. Next Hecuba made her lament. "Hector," she said, "you were the dearest to me of all my sons. The gods loved you when you were alive and even in death they have taken care of you. For though Achilles dragged you around the tomb of his friend, whom you killed, you lie now in your palace fresh as dew, comely and beautiful, like one whom Apollo of the Silver Bow has gently visited in death."

Again the women wept with her, and then Helen made the third lament. "Hector," she said, "since Paris brought me here to be his wife (and I wish I had perished first), you have always been much the dearest to me of all my brothers in Troy. It is nineteen years now since I came here and left my own country, and in all that time I have never once heard from you an unkind or an ungracious word. Others have reproached me—your brothers, your sisters, your mother (though never your father, who has been as kind to me as if I were his own child). But you always stopped them from insulting me, so gentle you were to me in your heart, so kind and courteous in your ways and words. And now I weep both for you and for my wretched self, since I have no one left in all Troy to be kind to me or to care for me. Instead they all shudder at the sight of me."

So Helen spoke, weeping. And now Priam gave orders for the preparation of the funeral. For nine days the Trojans mourned over Hector and meanwhile they brought into the city from the forests of Mount Ida great quantities of wood to make the funeral pyre. On the tenth day they put the body on the fire and set it alight, weeping as they did so. They collected the bones together, wrapped them in soft purple cloths and put them in a golden chest. Over the bones, on the eleventh day, they raised a great mound. Then they set sentries on the walls, in case the Greeks should attack before the time, and they went back to the palace of King Priam where the funeral feast was to be held.

Thus all the proper rites were performed at the burial of great Hector.

BOOK THREE

THE FALL OF TROY

I

THE DEATH OF ACHILLES

AFTER THE death of Hector it might well have seemed that the Trojans would be no longer able to resist Achilles and the victorious Greeks. Yet they were wisely led by Prince Aeneas, and by the few surviving sons of Priam. Moreover now, in the tenth year of the war, reinforcements were at hand. Two great new armies came to strengthen the defenders of Troy. The first of these armies was led by Memnon, the king of the Ethiopians, the second was an army of Amazons, the women who fight from horseback like men, and was led by the Amazon Queen Penthesilea.

King Memnon was the nephew of Priam, and, like Priam's other nephew Aeneas, he was the son of a goddess. His father was Tithonus, the son of Laomedon; but Tithonus had been carried up to heaven before the time of Laomedon's treachery to Herakles. Yet, as we shall see, though he was made immortal he was not made happy.

It was Aurora, goddess of the Dawn, who fell in love with young Tithonus, and used to rest with him in the woods and deep glades of Mount Ida. So much did she love him that she took him with her to her heavenly palace, and she begged Father Zeus to make him immortal. Zeus granted her prayer, but the prayer itself was an unwise one. Tithonus was indeed immortal, but she had forgotten to ask at the same time that he should remain, like the deathless gods, young and beautiful as he was. Thus, though Tithonus could not die, he did grow old, and, as he felt the weakness of age overcoming his limbs, as he saw the wrinkles on his face, dwelling day after day in the rosy palace of Aurora, he could not bear the thought of what he had been and of what he was. He begged Aurora to revoke her gift and to let him share the fate of all men and die. But even the gods cannot recall their gifts. So Tithonus grew older and older, more and more feeble in that splendid palace, losing his taste for sight and colours, for music, food and drink and every pleasure of his youth. In the end, they say, the gods had pity on him. Though they could not let him die, they changed his shape and turned him into a small insect, the cicada which sings merrily through the summer days among the trees and rocks.

But long before this time a son was born to Aurora and Tithonus. This son was Memnon who became king of the great nation of the Ethiopians. It was he who now led an army of ten thousand men to Troy, and both his army and his own presence, since he was a great warrior, encouraged the Trojans to renew the fighting. They fought on the more fiercely to preserve their homes and to avenge the death of Hector.

Memnon himself was not fated to live long, yet before he died, he won great glory. Many Greeks fell before his spear and before the spears of his Ethiopian warriors. In the front line of battle he killed with his own hand Antilochus, the gallant young son of Nestor and the friend of Achilles. At this loss the Greeks were sad indeed, yet the grief of none of them equalled the grief of old King Nestor himself. Distraught with longing for his son, he sent a challenge to Memnon, offering to fight with him in single combat. Memnon, however, was too chivalrous to use his great strength and his skill in arms against an old man still mourning for his dead son. Instead he chose to accept a challenge from Achilles, who also longed to avenge the friend whom he had loved. Yet not even Aurora could help

her son against Achilles. Though Memnon fought bravely
and well, his spear and sword could not pierce the imperishable armour of Hephaestus, and in the end he fell,
slain by the invincible hands that had destroyed Hector
and so many others.

Aurora wept for her son. She could not bring him to life
again any more than she could give youth back to her
husband; but she saved his dead body from Achilles and
she begged Zeus to show her son some honour at his funeral.
Zeus granted her prayer and, while the Trojans burned the
body of Memnon on a high pyre, a miracle took place. The
clouds of smoke that eddied up from the great fire that was
devouring the body began suddenly to take on distinct
shapes that looked different from smoke. As the onlookers
stared upwards in amazement, they saw the smoke changing
into the figures of birds. Soon the whole air was full of them;
the wheeling flock flew three times round the pyre, then
separated into two flocks which immediately began to fight
bitterly together. So fiercely did they attack each other that
nearly all of them were destroyed before they broke off the
battle and flew away. These birds came to be called "the
birds of Memnon" and for generations afterwards they
would come each year on the same day to renew their
battle over Memnon's tomb. So Zeus did honour to the son
of Aurora, and in Memnon's own country the Ethiopians
raised for him a wonderful and gigantic statue which had the
power of making sounds. At dawn when the sun's first rays
fell upon this statue, it would seem to speak in a melodious
voice and in the evening, when the sun set, it would make a
noise that was more like the noise of mourning.

So, even after his death, the name of Memnon remained
famous on the earth, and round Troy the fighting continued
as bitterly as before. The army of the Amazons, fierce
women armed with double-headed axes, pressed the Greeks
hard, but here again the Greeks were delivered by Achilles
who, coming to close quarters, slew Penthesilea, the Amazon

queen, with his sword. They say that when he stripped the armour from her body he was astonished at her beauty and wept for what he had done. Yet now his own fate was close upon him. As he led the victorious Greeks forward, streaming towards the Scaean Gate, the moment came which had been fixed for him at birth by the Fates. Though for long he had been irresistible, now he was in the hands of the gods, and though he expected that day to sack the city of Troy, once more the city was saved by Apollo. It was Paris who shot the arrow that killed great Achilles, but Apollo strengthened the archer's arm and directed the arrow to that part of the body where alone it would bring death. Achilles fell in the dust in front of the Scaean Gate, as Hector with his dying words had foretold, and the Greeks were dismayed when they saw their champion fall. Eagerly the Trojans surged forward to take the armour and the body of their great enemy and at first they forced the Greeks backwards in the fight. But Odysseus stood firm, and while he beat off every attack that the Trojans made upon him, great Ajax rescued the body and carried it back to the ships. Afterwards it was decided that the splendid armour of Achilles should be given either to Ajax or to Odysseus, since they had been friends of Achilles, had saved his body in the fighting and were among the greatest of the Greeks. There was much debate as to which of the two was most worthy of the armour, but in the end Agamemnon, Menelaus and the other leaders decided that it should be given to Odysseus. And now Ajax, great warrior though he was, could not bear what he considered was an unjust decision. He went out of his mind and fell upon a herd of sheep, imagining them to be the two sons of Atreus and the other generals who had awarded the armour to Odysseus. In his madness, he slaughtered these animals, and then, when he came again to his right mind, he was ashamed at what he had done and killed himself with his own sword, preferring to die rather than to live with the memory of how he had lost his wits and disgraced his own great name. The Greeks built him a high monument on the shore and in his own country of Salamis he was honoured ever afterwards for his strength and for his steadfastness in battle.

But first the Greeks mourned for Achilles as bitterly as the Trojans had mourned for Hector. By the sea coast and near the ships they raised for him a high mound where his bones were buried together with the bones of his friend Patroclus. His mother Thetis with her sisters, the nymphs of the sea, came to mourn at his funeral and the Greeks honoured their dead leader as though he was a god.

Old King Peleus did not know yet of his son's death and iust before had allowed his grandson, Neoptolemus, the young son of Achilles, to sail himself to Troy that he might fight beside his father. But when Neoptolemus arrived, he found that of his great father nothing was left except the high funeral mound and an undying fame. Neoptolemus wept at Achilles' tomb, and then he flung himself fiercely into the war, soon showing himself to be a warrior worthy of his birth.

So the fighting continued and still the blood of men stained the waters of the River Scamander or was soaked up in the dusty ground.

II

THE FATAL HORSE

CALCHAS, THE prophet, had foretold that the war would end in the tenth year, yet still the war dragged on, still the Trojans, led by Aeneas and by Paris, fought on behind their walls or in front of their city, and still the Greeks, for all that they could do, failed to win a decisive advantage.

And now another prophecy was made known to the army. Some say that it was again Calchas who made the revelation; some say that Odysseus and Diomedes captured Helenus, a son of Priam and the chief prophet of the Trojans, and that it was he who revealed to them that Troy would never be captured without the famous bow and arrows of Herakles. These were in possession of the warrior Philoctetes, whom the Greeks had cruelly abandoned on the island of Lemnos nine years before this time. On this rocky island Philoctetes remained, still suffering from the wound he had received from the bite of a snake, in continual pain and in continual anger with the Greeks who had deserted him.

Now in their great need the Greeks were ashamed of the cruelty with which they had treated this great warrior. Odysseus and Neoptolemus went to Lemnos in order to urge Philoctetes to return with them and to give them his help. They found him weak and tortured by the pain of his wound which had so corrupted his flesh that all men avoided him because of the dreadful smell of decay with which he was surrounded. At first he refused utterly to come to the help of the Greeks. And indeed the young Neoptolemus was so deeply affected by the story of his sufferings that he was prepared, against the wishes of Odysseus, to help Philoctetes to escape from the island and to return to his own country. But, just as this plan was about to be carried out, Philoctetes saw in a vision the great Herakles himself who, after his many labours, had become a god. Herakles ordered him to forgive his enemies and to sail at once to Troy, where the Greek physician Machaon would cure him of his wound.

So Philoctetes obeyed and went with Odysseus and Neoptolemus to the Greek camp, where Agamemnon and the rest received him with honour and gave him that share of the spoils which would have been his if he had been with the army from the beginning of the war. His wound was cured by Machaon who had the skill and the soothing ointments of his great father, Asclepius, the best of all doctors. Then Philoctetes, armed with the bow of Herakles, entered the battle, and among the many who fell to his arrows was Paris, the son of Priam, who was the cause of the whole war. Paris was not killed immediately by the arrow with which Philoctetes struck him, but he was mortally wounded and there was no doctor in Troy who could heal his wound. So he gave orders to his servants that he should be carried to Mount Ida to the nymph Oenone whom he had loved and who had loved him in the days before he was visited by the three goddesses and made the fatal judgment. Oenone had great skill in medicine and knew the virtues of all healing herbs. Messengers went in front of Paris to find the nymph and to beg her to assist her old lover in his extreme peril; but she was still angry with Paris for having deserted her and she refused to give him her help. When the messengers returned and told him of her refusal, Paris knew that he had no hope left. In a weak voice he ordered the men who were carrying him to turn back, so that he might die in Troy, and, when he was brought to his own palace, he had scarcely the strength to say farewell to his father and his mother and to Helen, for whose sake he was about to die. So he died in his bed of a wound from one of the arrows of Herakles. And no sooner was he dead than the nymph Oenone came to the city, having repented of the words she had spoken to the messengers that Paris had sent to her. Since they had left her, she had changed her mind and now she was ready to employ all her skill in attempting to save his life. But she had come too late. Paris was dead. It seems, however, that, though he had treated her most cruelly, she still loved him, for, at the sight of his dead body, she stabbed herself with her own hand and fell lifeless at his side.

Paris had caused the war in which better men than he had lost their lives, and now that he was dead there might have been, perhaps, some hope of peace. But by this time nothing would satisfy the Greeks except the total destruction of Troy and, though the war had been started for Helen's sake, they would never have laid down their arms even if Helen with all her goods were restored to them. Yet though they fought on to avenge their own dead and to reach final victory, victory still escaped them, and in the end it was not by fighting but by a stratagem that the city was taken and the race of Priam utterly destroyed.

It was Odysseus who made the plan which was to lead to the fall of Troy. Under his orders the Greeks made out of wood the figure of a huge horse. The face and nostrils of the horse, its feet and hooves were beautifully carved. Its body was hollow and was of such a size that twenty armed men could hide within it. And this is what they did. Odysseus himself with Diomedes, Menelaus, Neoptolemus and others of the best of the Greeks climbed inside the wooden framework of the horse's gigantic body and there they waited fully armed, knowing that this desperate venture would end either in their own deaths or in the destruction of Troy.

For while these great warriors lay hidden inside the horse, Agamemnon, with the rest of the Greek army, had embarked on their ships by night and sailed away. They sailed just as far as the shelter of the island of Tenedos, which lies some twelve miles distant from the Trojan coast. There the fleet was out of sight, and when dawn came and the Trojan sentries reported that the Greek camp was deserted, all the Trojans believed that their enemies, exhausted and dispirited by their sufferings, had sailed back to Greece, abandoning finally the purpose of their great expedition. It was a day of joy and gratitude in Troy. The people came out of the city, singing and dancing and offering thanks to the gods for what they imagined was their deliverance. They came to the deserted shore where the Greek camp had been and looked at the huts, now empty, where famous men—Achilles, Agamemnon, Diomedes and Odysseus—had lived for so long. In particular they wondered at the huge wooden horse and made all kinds of guesses as to the purpose for which it had been made. Many of the Trojans wished at once to drag the horse inside the walls of their city, so that it might stay there for ever as a trophy and sign of their victory. There were others however who were in favour of hurling it into the sea or setting fire to it, so that there should be nothing left on the Trojan coast which could possibly remind them of the Greeks. Chief among those who wished to destroy the horse was Laocoön, the priest of Apollo. "Trojans," he cried out to the people, "have you taken leave of your senses? How can you be sure yet that our enemies have gone away? Is this what you would expect of Odysseus or of Diomedes? I believe that this horse has been made to deceive us. Either there are armed men inside, or else it is some kind of a machine which can be used against our walls. Whatever it is, I for my part still distrust all Greeks, even when they seem to be offering us gifts."

As he spoke he poised a spear and hurled it at the horse. The point stuck in the wood and the shaft quivered. A hollow sound came from the body and now, if the Trojans had not been blinded by the gods, they would have sawn through the wood and explored the hiding places within. So they would have saved their city and the high palaces of Priam. But this was not to be. And now other events were to confirm them in their folly.

When the Greeks had sailed away, they left behind them one man, named Sinon, promising him a great reward and instructing him to tell a false story so that the Trojans would take the horse inside their walls. Now this man Sinon, who had given himself up to a patrol of Trojan soldiers, was brought by them, with his hands tied behind his back, in front of the chief men of Troy. Sinon told his story well. He pretended that he was an enemy of Odysseus and that Odysseus had planned to take his life. Therefore, he said, he had been forced to hide from the Greeks and to throw himself on the mercy of the Trojans. As he spoke of his pretended sufferings, he wept what seemed to be real tears, and there were few who did not believe what he said. As for the horse, he told them that it was an offering which the Greeks had been commanded to make to the goddess Athene. If the Trojans were to destroy it, that would mean certain destruction for their city; but if they took it inside their walls, they would always have the protection of Athene and, in course of time, they would invade Greece itself and conquer the sons or the grandsons of those who had fought against them for so long. Calchas, the prophet, had warned the Greeks of this and it was for this reason that they had made the horse so big, in order that it should be difficult for the Trojans to drag it inside their walls.

This story of Sinon's was believed and so the Trojans who had resisted Achilles and Diomedes and an expedition of a thousand ships, became the victims of a cunning plot. Still further were they deceived by the gods, for now Zeus no longer protected the city which he had loved and he allowed those gods and goddesses who hated Troy and the race of Priam to have their own way and to act as seemed best to them. Now either Athene or Poseidon sent monsters out of the sea in order to make the Trojans doubt the good advice that had been given to them by Laocoön.

The priest, accompanied by his two young sons, was sacrificing on the shore, when far out in the blue water there appeared two huge snakes swimming strongly towards the land with their blood-red heads projecting above the level surface of the sea. Soon they were on the beach and here they paused for a moment; their forked tongues flickered in and out of their mouths as they stared about them with blazing and with blood-shot eyes. Then they made straight for Laocoön and first the snakes twined themselves round the bodies of the priest's sons, crushing the boys to death in their huge and scaly folds. The wretched father hurried to the help of his sons, and then the snakes wound their coils about him too. In vain he tried to free himself; they pinned his arms to his sides and choked him as they coiled about his neck. Soon he lay dead beside the bodies of his sons, and then the snakes fled to the city of Troy and took refuge in the temple of Athene.

Now indeed the Trojans were confirmed in their wrong opinions. Everyone said that this fate had come upon Laocoön because he had insulted the goddess by hurling his spear at the horse which was sacred to her. Men, women and children hurried to bring the fatal horse into the city. Ropes were fastened to its neck; the ground was cleared so that it would be easier to drag, and hymns of praise were sung while this monstrous effigy, bearing inside it the best warriors of the Greeks, was taken into the doomed town. So big was the horse that it was necessary to destroy part of the walls near the gate in order that it should have room to enter. No one then thought of how these walls had preserved the Trojans for so long. Instead there was nothing but cheering and rejoicing, a noise that drowned the noise of clashing armour which came from inside the horse when three times it stuck on the very threshold of the city.

Here once more the Trojans were warned of the fate which was hanging over them. Priam's daughter Cassandra had been given the power of prophecy by Apollo himself, but later she had deceived the god and the god had become angry with her. He could not take away his gift, but he made it worthless. Cassandra indeed always prophesied truly, but Apollo made those who heard her always disbelieve her. Now once more she warned the Trojans of their folly, and once more no one paid any attention to her warnings.

So the horse was brought within the walls of Troy and all day the Trojans gave themselves up to feasting and rejoicing. Far into the night their feast continued; no sentries were posted on the walls or along the coast. Confident in their security and tired out from their exertions and their rejoicings, at length they slept in a city that was already almost in their enemies' hands.

For as soon as all was quiet, Sinon made his way to the place where the horse stood. He undid the cunningly contrived bolts, and pulled the timbers apart. Moonlight shone on the eager and expectant faces of the Greeks within, who now gripped their arms, descended from their place of concealment and went quietly through the sleeping city to the gates.

Meanwhile Agamemnon with the whole fleet had set sail from Tenedos. In the silent moonlight they had drawn their ships up on the beach that they knew so well. Silently they had crossed the plain, and now, when Odysseus, Diomedes and the rest opened the city gates to them, they joined forces together and swept into Troy, killing and burning as they went. Almost before the Trojans could arm themselves and long before they could make any plans for defence, the city was lost, high towers were crumbling in ruin and tall flames shooting upwards to the sky. In the moment of their triumph the Greeks showed mercy neither to young nor old. Small children and white-haired men were butchered in the streets and in their very beds. So great was the hatred that this long war had provoked, so bitter and outrageous the feelings of those who were at last victorious.

III

THE ESCAPE OF AENEAS

PRINCE AENEAS had gone to sleep that night in the home of his old father Anchises, a palace that lay back from the streets in a quiet and secluded quarter of the city. As he slept there came to him, whether as a dream or in a vision, the ghost of great Hector. He seemed to stand there before Aeneas's eyes and, as he stood, his face was wet with tears. All the wounds that he had received in defending Troy and in his last fight with Achilles were clearly visible on his body. His hair was matted together and covered with dust; his feet were pierced by the cruel wounds that Achilles had made before he dragged the body behind his chariot.

At the sight Aeneas himself wept or dreamed that he was weeping. He spoke first and said: "O Hector, you who were the light of Troy and our great defender, from where have you come, and what is it that has disturbed your calm face? Why do you appear with these wounds upon you?"

Hector heaved a deep sigh. He looked earnestly at Aeneas and said "Alas! my friend, I have come to tell you to escape. Our walls are in the hands of the enemy. The city is on fire. Great Troy is falling. But you are fated to take the gods of Troy and to found in another country another city. So in the end from your Trojan blood there will come a power even greater than the power of Priam or of Agamemnon. Here in our own country there will be nothing but ruin and desolation; but, after many wanderings, you will find a place to rest and there Troy will be reborn."

With these words Hector vanished and Aeneas woke with the voice ringing in his head. He sprang up and went out on to the roof of the palace. There he stood still in dumb astonishment, for in all directions he saw the blaze of fires. Not far distant the great palace of Deiphobus, the son of Priam, was crashing to the ground in swirling sheets of flame. All the sky was lit up and the far away waters of the sea glowed red in the dreadful illumination. Then from all sides came the shrieks of women and children, the sound of trumpets, shouting and the clashing of arms.

True indeed were the words of Hector. These were the last hours of Troy. This was the end of the great glory of Priam and of the Trojan name. The Greeks were masters of the burning city.

Yet Aeneas did not at once do as Hector had told him and make his escape. Hurriedly he armed himself and rushed out into the streets. Fury gave him strength and courage, so that he was resolved, if he could not save the city, at least to die fighting with the conquerors. Soon he gathered together a small band of Trojans who were as willing to fight as he was, and with them he made his way through the burning streets towards the great palace of Priam. As they went they fell upon every party of Greeks whom they met, nor was there anyone that night who could stand before the spear of Aeneas. He fought like a lion and was determined to fight on until his strength failed him or the weight of numbers bore him down.

So they reached the palace of Priam. Here everything was in confusion. Half the palace was in flames and beyond the flames the main army of the Greeks was surging forward, battering down the doors, killing the men and dragging off the women as prisoners. Beyond the burning buildings Aeneas saw the beautiful daughter of Priam, Cassandra, being dragged away by her hair. She was destined to be the slave of Agamemnon. Agamemnon himself and Menelaus were at the threshold of the inner chambers, shouting orders

THE END OF TROY

to their men. And closer at hand was a more terrible sight; for through the flames they could see old Priam clinging to the altar at his own hearthstone. Yet the holy altar could not preserve his life. Fierce Neoptolemus burst open the door, dragged the old man away from the place where he was seeking refuge and butchered him with his sharp sword. Then with one blow he severed the head from the body. So fate came to King Priam. He saw his city on fire, his palace falling to the ground, his daughters and his wife carried away into slavery and all his sons slain by the Greeks. He who had been the master of Asia, ruling over so many cities and peoples, now lay stretched out in his own blood, a huge body, without a head and without a name.

Aeneas looked at the sight with horror. His first impulse was to dash into the flames and either die there or die beyond them in battle with the Greeks; but then there came to his mind the thought of his own old father Anchises and of his wife Creusa and of his son Ascanius whom he had left behind in his palace. He turned back, resolved to protect them if he could or at least to share their fate.

On his way through the ruined palace he saw in the light of the flames Helen sitting by herself, in fear both of the Trojans and of the Greeks. And now the heart of Aeneas was filled with burning anger. It was because of her, he thought, that Troy, with its high towers, was going up in flames, because of her that Hector had died and that old Priam lay butchered on his own hearth. Why should she, who had done such evil to the men and women of Troy, be allowed to escape and to return to her own country? He drew his sword and was already moving towards her when suddenly there appeared to him the goddess, his mother, Aphrodite in her full splendour as she is seen by the gods themselves. She took his hand gently and spoke to him. "My son," she said, "you are being carried away by madness. Your first care should be for your old father, for your wife and for the little Ascanius. Up to now I have preserved them, but now it is for you to go to their help. And it is not because of Helen, nor because of Paris that Troy is falling. It is the gods themselves who are unmerciful, and strong fate that is bringing this city to destruction. See, I will take away the veil from your eyes, so that you may know that now there is no human power which could save Troy from the great gods who are its enemies."

As she spoke Aeneas seemed to see behind the raging forces of the Greeks the figures of enormous gods. Poseidon, the Earth-shaker, was tearing down the walls. Clouds of dust and the roar of falling masonry followed every blow of his tremendous trident. At the Scaean Gate was the goddess Hera, urging on the Greeks to slaughter and to rapine; and on the high citadel stood Pallas Athene with a fierce light blazing from her terrible shield and breastplate.

Aeneas turned back to his divine mother, but she herself had disappeared. And now it seemed to him that the whole of Troy was crashing to the ground among the burning flames, like some great tree which, for long shaken by the blows of felling axes, in the end totters, while the topmost branches shiver, and then finally with a splintering crash falls and spreads its ruin over the ground.

So Aeneas obeyed his mother Aphrodite and went back to his father's house through the flames and through the lines of the enemy. But when he reached the place and explained to old Anchises his plan of escape to the mountains, the old man refused to go. "Go yourself, my son," he said, "and take with you your wife and child. I have lived here too long. Already I am worn out with age and I wish to die with the city where all my life has been spent."

"How could I bear to go," Aeneas replied, "and leave you here to be killed as I saw Priam killed? No. If your mind is made up, I shall die here with you, though first I shall bring death and vengeance on our enemies."

So saying, he fitted the shield to his arm and took his spear in his hand. But first he prepared to say farewell to his wife Creusa and to his small son Ascanius, who were weeping in sorrow and in terror.

And now a miracle happened. Suddenly from the top of the head of Ascanius a bright flame began to spring up. It burned clearly and lapped the whole forehead of the boy with fire, yet the fire did not scorch his skin. Old Anchises stretched out his hands and prayed, as he looked up to the sky. "Almighty Zeus, if my prayer can reach you, look down on us and help us. Show us what is the meaning of this sign."

Hardly had he spoken when Zeus clearly revealed his will. There was a clap of thunder on the left and then, as they stared upwards, they saw a bright shooting star running across the sky. It crossed directly over the top of their house and then plunged to earth in the forests of Mount Ida, lighting up the trees and showing them the way on which they should go.

Now Anchises hesitated no longer. "My son," he said, "lead the way and I will go with you. O gods of my country, save this house and save my grandson. Troy will be restored in him and in his descendants."

Hurriedly then they took their flight. The old man was too feeble to walk, so Aeneas carried him on his shoulders. The little boy Ascanius clung to his hand and his wife Creusa followed in his footsteps. To the comrades who were still with him Aeneas gave orders to make their own way out of the burning city and to meet him beyond the city walls at the sacred mound in the plain below the slopes of Mount Ida. Then Aeneas himself with his family set out, seeking the cover of darkness where there was any darkness; and now Aeneas, with the precious burden on his back and clasping his son's hand, moved cautiously, fearing the slightest sound, though at other times he had never feared the roar of battle but had always gone forward against the enemy.

So he escaped and, coming to the mound, found all his comrades gathered there. But there was one who was even more than a comrade to him who was missing. When at last he turned back to look for her, he saw that Creusa, his wife, was not there. In vain he cursed himself for not having made sure all the time that she was following him; in vain he tried to remember where on the way she might have lost sight of him in some dark alley or have been overcome with weariness; in vain he questioned his companions. No one had seen her. It seemed that some fate had snatched her from him.

So Aeneas put his father and his son into the care of his companions, while he himself went back again among the flames to look for his wife. Carefully he retraced his steps as far as his own house. He found the house on fire and the Greeks surrounding it. He saw the long processions of captured women and all the Trojan treasures being gathered together for division by the victorious Greeks. He saw the marks of blood and of violence on every side. Still he went on searching for his wife and crying out her name in the darkened streets where she might have taken refuge. Then suddenly before his eyes he saw not her, but her ghost. She had the same gentle expression in her eyes, but she seemed bigger and taller than she was in life and a strange light shone from her face. "Dear husband," she said to him, "you must not mourn for me and you must not risk your life any longer in searching for me. All this has happened by the will of the gods, who do not wish you to take me away with you. Zeus himself has other plans for you. You will have many years of wandering and will cross a great waste of surging sea. In the end you will come to Italy in the far West and there by the river Tiber you will found a city and you will have a royal bride. Do not weep for Creusa whom you loved. I shall not fall into the hands of the Greeks. The gods are taking care of me, but now your fate is separate from mine. Farewell, dear husband, and remember me in the love you feel for our child."

She ceased speaking and disappeared into the thin air,

though Aeneas longed to speak more to her and to hear her voice again. Three times he tried to fold her in his arms, but each time she slipped from his embrace, like a breath of air or like a fleeting dream.

Then Aeneas went back to his father and his son and his companions who were destined with him to save the great name of Troy and to found, after many adventures, a city in the West from which would come in due time a race of heroes, used to danger and to difficulty, who would build the high walls of Rome.

Meanwhile in the captured city all was havoc and destruction. The wives and the daughters of kings now passed as slaves into the victors' hands. Little Astyanax, the son of Hector, was killed, as his mother had feared, by a Greek maddened with hatred for the loss of some brother or friend slain by the spear of his great father. In their victory the Greeks forgot the difference between right and wrong. They were cruel and unmerciful, often not sparing even the temples of the gods. Thus the gods themselves were angry with them. Sufferings awaited them on their voyage home and in their very homes when they reached them.

So ended the great expedition against Troy.

TITLES IN THE NEW WINDMILL SERIES

Chinua Achebe: *Things Fall Apart*
Louisa M. Alcott: *Little Women*
Elizabeth Allen: *Deitz and Denny*
Margery Allingham: *The Tiger in the Smoke*
Michael Anthony: *The Year in San Fernando*
Enid Bagnold: *National Velvet*
Stan Barstow: *Joby*
H. Mortimer Batten: *The Singing Forest*
Nina Bawden: *On the Run; The Witch's Daughter; A Handful of Thieves; Carrie's War; Rebel on a Rock*
Rex Benedict: *Last Stand at Goodbye Gulch*
Phyllis Bentley: *The Adventures of Tom Leigh*
Paul Berna: *Flood Warning*
Pierre Boulle: *The Bridge on the River Kwai*
E. R. Braithwaite: *To Sir, With Love*
D. K. Broster: *The Flight of the Heron; The Gleam in the North*
F. Hodgson Burnett: *The Secret Garden*
Helen Bush: *Mary Anning's Treasures*
A. Calder-Marshall: *The Man from Devil's Island*
John Caldwell: *Desperate Voyage*
Albert Camus: *The Outsider*
Victor Canning: *The Runaways; Flight of the Grey Goose*
Erskine Childers: *The Riddle of the Sands*
John Christopher: *The Guardians; The Lotus Caves*
Richard Church: *The Cave; Over the Bridge; The White Doe*
Colette: *My Mother's House*
Alexander Cordell: *The Traitor Within*
Margaret Craven: *I Heard the Owl Call my Name*
Roald Dahl: *Danny, Champion of the World; The Wonderful Story of Henry Sugar*
Meindert deJong: *The Wheel on the School*
Peter Dickinson: *The Gift; Annerton Pit*
Eleanor Doorly: *The Radium Woman; The Microbe Man; The Insect Man*
Gerald Durrell: *Three Singles to Adventure; The Drunken Forest; Encounters with Animals*
Elizabeth Enright: *Thimble Summer; The Saturdays*
C. S. Forester: *The General*
Eve Garnett: *The Family from One End Street; Further Adventures of the Family from One End Street; Holiday at the Dew Drop Inn*
G. M. Glaskin: *A Waltz through the Hills*
Rumer Godden: *Black Narcissus*
Angus Graham: *The Golden Grindstone*
Graham Greene: *The Third Man* and *The Fallen Idol*
Grey Owl: *Sajo and her Beaver People*
John Griffin: *Skulker Wheat and Other Stories*
G. and W. Grossmith: *The Diary of a Nobody*
René Guillot: *Kpo the Leopard*
Esther Hautzig: *The Endless Steppe*
Jan De Hartog: *The Lost Sea*
Erik Haugaard: *The Little Fishes*
Bessie Head: *When Rain Clouds Gather*
Ernest Hemingway: *The Old Man and the Sea*
John Hersey: *A Single Pebble*
Georgette Heyer: *Regency Buck*

Alfred Hitchcock: *Sinister Spies*

C. Walter Hodges: *The Overland Launch*

Geoffrey Household: *Rogue Male; A Rough Shoot; Prisoner of the Indies; Escape into Daylight*

Fred Hoyle: *The Black Cloud*

Irene Hunt: *Across Five Aprils*

Henry James: *Washington Square*

Josephine Kamm: *Young Mother; Out of Step; Where Do We Go From Here?; The Starting Point*

Erich Kästner: *Emil and the Detectives; Lottie and Lisa*

Clive King: *Me and My Million*

John Knowles: *A Separate Peace*

D. H. Lawrence: *Sea and Sardinia; The Fox* and *The Virgin and the Gipsy; Selected Tales*

Marghanita Laski: *Little Boy Lost*

Harper Lee: *To Kill a Mockingbird*

Laurie Lee: *As I Walked Out One Mid-Summer Morning*

Ursula Le Guin: *A Wizard of Earthsea; The Tombs of Atuan; The Farthest Shore; A Very Long Way from Anywhere Else*

Doris Lessing: *The Grass is Singing*

C. Day Lewis: *The Otterbury Incident*

Lorna Lewis: *Leonardo the Inventor*

Martin Lindsay: *The Epic of Captain Scott*

David Line: *Run for Your Life; Mike and Me*

Kathleen Lines: *The House of the Nightmare; The Haunted and the Haunters*

Joan Lingard: *Across the Barricades; Into Exile; The Clearance*

Penelope Lively: *The Ghost of Thomas Kempe*

Jack London: *The Call of the Wild; White Fang*

Carson McCullers: *The Member of the Wedding*

Lee McGiffen: *On the Trail to Sacramento*

Wolf Mankowitz: *A Kid for Two Farthings*

Olivia Manning: *The Play Room*

Jan Mark: *Thunder and Lightnings*

James Vance Marshall: *A River Ran Out of Eden; Walkabout; My Boy John that Went to Sea*

David Martin: *The Cabby's Daughter*

J. P. Martin: *Uncle*

John Masefield: *The Bird of Dawning; The Midnight Folk; The Box of Delights*

W. Somerset Maugham: *The Kite and Other Stories*

Guy de Maupassant: *Prisoners of War and Other Stories*

Laurence Meynell: *Builder and Dreamer*

Yvonne Mitchell: *Cathy Away*

Honoré Morrow: *The Splendid Journey*

Bill Naughton: *The Goalkeeper's Revenge; A Dog Called Nelson; My Pal Spadger*

E. Nesbit: *The Railway Children; The Story of the Treasure Seekers*

E. Neville: *It's Like this, Cat*

Wilfrid Noyce: *South Col*

Robert C. O'Brien: *Mrs Frisby and the Rats of NIMH; Z for Zachariah*

Scott O'Dell: *Island of the Blue Dolphins*

George Orwell: *Animal Farm*

K. M. Peyton: *Flambards*

Philippa Pearce: *Tom's Midnight Garden*

John Prebble: *The Buffalo Soldiers*